CHARLES F. STANLEY B

EXPERIENCING FORGIVENESS

ENJOY THE PEACE OF
GIVING AND RECEIVING GRACE

CHARLES F. STANLEY

Experiencing Forgiveness
Charles F. Stanley Bible Study Series

Published in Nashville, Tennessee, by Thomas Nelson. Thomas Nelson is a registered trademark of HarperCollins Christian Publishing, Inc.

Thomas Nelson titles may be purchased in bulk for educational, business, fundraising, or sales promotional use. For information, e-mail SpecialMarkets@ThomasNelson.com.

ISBN 978-0-310-10657-9

First Printing August 2019 / Printed in the United States of America

HB 01.10.2024

CONTENTS

INTRODUCTION

God's Perspective on Forgiveness

Each of us has a perspective on the world and on life—a way of looking at things, of judging things, of holding things in our memories We need to recognize that our perspective is something we have learned, and we need to recognize we may have adopted a wrong understanding about certain things.

I have found in my years of ministry that a wrong perspective is very common when it comes to the matter of forgiveness. Many of us have misconceptions about why God forgives us, who God forgives, what it means to be forgiven, and how we are to go about being forgiven and forgiving ourselves and others.

For the right perspective on forgiveness, we must go to God's Word and stay there. The Bible is God's foremost communication to us on this subject. It is the reference to which we must return continually to compare what is happening in us with what should be happening in us. Our perspective is wrong anytime it doesn't match up with God's eternal truth.

This book can be used by you alone or by several people in a small-group study. At various times, you will be asked to relate to the material in one of the following four ways.

First, what new insights have you gained? Make notes about these insights as God reveals them to you, recording them in your Bible or in a separate journal. As you reflect on these new understandings, you are more likely to see how God has moved in your life.

Second, how do you relate to the material? You approach the Bible from your own unique background . . . your own particular set of understandings about the world that you bring with you when you open God's Word. For this reason, it is important to consider how your experiences are shaping your understanding and allow yourself to be open to the truth that God reveals—even if it isn't necessary what you expect. As you do this, you allow God's Word to be a lamp to your feet and a light to your path (see Psalm 119:105).

Third, how do you feel about the material presented? While you should not depend solely on your emotions as a gauge for your faith, it is important for you to be aware of your feelings as you study a passage of Scripture and have the freedom to express your emotions to God. Sometimes, the Holy Spirit will use your emotions to compel you to look at your life in a different or challenging way.

Fourth, in what way do you feel challenged to respond? God's Word may inspire you or challenge you to take a particular action. Take this challenge seriously and find ways to move into it. If God reveals a particular need He wants *you* to address, take that as His "marching orders." God will empower you to *do* something with the challenge He has just given you.

Start and conclude your Bible study sessions in prayer. Ask God to give you spiritual eyes to see and spiritual ears to hear. As you conclude your study, ask the Lord to seal what you have learned so that you will never forget it. Ask Him to help you grow into the fullness of the stature of Christ Jesus.

Again, I caution you to keep the Bible at the center of your study. A genuine Bible study stays focused on God's Word and promotes a growing faith and a closer walk with the Holy Spirit in each person who participates.

LESSON 1

GOD HAS A PURPOSE FOR EVERYTHING

IN THIS LESSON

Learning: What exactly is forgiveness?

Growing: How can I stop being an unforgiving person?

"Forgive me? How could God ever forgive me? You don't know what I've done." "Forgive that person after what she did to me? You've got to be kidding!" "I can't believe I've done such an awful thing. I can never forgive myself for doing that."

These are confessions I hear often as a pastor. They are the confessions of people who have godly parents, have grown up in church, and have heard sermons about forgiveness all their lives. Yet they persist in believing there is something unique about their situation that puts them beyond God's forgiveness. The result is bondage.

This bondage of living in guilt and unforgiveness stifles their ability to love and receive love. It stunts the growth of their marriages and friendships. It keeps them from entering into all the Lord might have for them in the way of ministry or outreach. It keeps them from enjoying the full abundant life that Christ promised to those who believe in Him (see John 10:10). Bondage is never the desire of God for His children.

God's desire is that you be free in your spirit—free to embrace the blessings, challenges, and joys He has for you now and in your future. God's desire is for you to experience *complete* forgiveness, which is forgiveness of your sins, a full restoration in your relationship with Him, forgiveness of others who have wronged you, and forgiveness of yourself.

Limited forgiveness will never do. Complete forgiveness on your part is required if you are to know personally and fully that God is your loving heavenly Father—and if you are ever to reach your personal destiny in this life.

1. When are times in your life that you struggled with issues of forgiveness and unforgiveness?

2. Have you experienced God's forgiveness in your life? Have you experienced forgiveness from someone else? Explain.

What Forgiveness Does Not Mean

At the outset of this study, we must define what forgiveness is not. *First, forgiveness does not mean, "It didn't matter."* If you have been hurt by someone, or if you have committed a sin, it *does* matter. There is no justification for sin that stands up in God's presence. If you have sinned, you need to recognize your sin is a blot on your soul—one that you can't and therefore shouldn't attempt to sweep under the rug or ignore. Sin matters. Hurt, pain, bondage, and guilt come in the aftermath of sin, and you are unwise to deny their reality.

Second, forgiveness does not mean, "I'll get over it in time." The memory of a particular incident or action may fade with time, but it never disappears. If you have committed a sin before God, the effects of that sin remain in your life until you receive God's forgiveness for it. You may not immediately feel the consequences of your sin—which can cause you to think God has overlooked your sin or it has been resolved in some way—but the consequences of sin will manifest themselves. They lie as dormant "bad seeds" in your life.

The same holds true for a wrong that another person commits against you. You may think that time will heal, but time by itself won't heal anything. Only the Lord Jesus Christ and His forgiveness working in and through your situation can heal the hurt that you have felt. A wrong you attempt to bury will only rot in your heart and can easily turn into bitterness, anger, and hatred. All of these are destructive emotions to the person who harbors them as well as the root of destructive behavior that may affect others.

Third, forgiveness does not mean, "There will be no penalty." Some people believe God skips over certain sins when He surveys the hearts of people. This is usually the response of those who hope God will make a detour around their sin and they'll get away with it.

There are other times, however, when we are fearful God will forget to discipline those who have wronged us. They may even seem to be prospering, and we feel a need to hold on to our unforgiveness until we are certain that they will be punished in some way. We hold on to the prerogative of vengeance "just in case" God has forgotten about the incident or intends to do nothing about it. At other times, we know we deserve to be punished, but God doesn't seem to be taking any action against us, so we refuse to forgive ourselves as a form of self-punishment.

These definitions don't hold water when they are subjected to the truth of God's Word. Sin matters. It *always* matters. Sin and the effects of sin don't disappear over time of their own accord. Sin *always* has consequences. It always bears with it the ultimate penalty of death.

3. What are some misunderstandings you've had in the past about forgiveness? What is the danger in thinking "you will just get over it in time" if someone hurts you?

4. Why is it important to remember that God doesn't just "skip over" another person's sin? Why is that important to remember in regard to your own sins?

What Forgiveness Does Mean

What then is forgiveness? *Forgiveness* is the act of setting someone free from an obligation to you that is a result of a wrong done against you. It involves three elements:

- *An injury.* A wrong is committed. Pain, hurt, suffering, or guilt is experienced (consciously or unconsciously).
- *A debt resulting from the injury.* There is a consequence that is always detrimental and puts someone into a deficit state of some kind.
- *A cancellation of the debt.* Forgiveness involves the conscious act of choosing not to hold the obligation against the other person.

We will be looking at each of these elements in greater depth in this study. All three are involved in forgiveness of all types—forgiveness by God, forgiveness of others, and forgiveness of self.

5. "Owe no one anything except to love one another, for he who loves another has fulfilled the law" (Romans 13:8). What kind of "debt" does Paul say is acceptable for believers in Christ to have toward others?

6. "Now it is high time to awake out of sleep; for now our salvation is nearer than when we first believed" (Romans 13:11). What reason does Paul state here for choosing to cancel our debts toward others and walk with Christ?

Unforgiven People

People who haven't received God's forgiveness are in pain. There is a festering wound in the soul. There is a wall in the spirit that keeps them imprisoned. They may not recognize they are in a state of unforgiveness, but many people who feel frustrated, burdened, impatient, angry, jealous, or bitter are victims of unforgiveness.

There are many people today who go through life in a state of bitterness, anxiety, and resentment. I've even met a few people who have gone through several years in their life of unforgiveness only to discover the person whom they thought wronged them was not the offender. Imagine that! Look what they carried with them. How many years of resentment, hostility, and anger did they harbor toward someone else—only to find they had the wrong person in mind! In the end, who suffered? *They* suffered. It doesn't make any difference if we have the right person or the wrong person. We always suffer when there is unforgiveness.

When we refuse to forgive, we break fellowship with God. This is why the Scriptures command that we lay our grievances down and lay them aside. "There we also, since we are surrounded by so great a cloud of witnesses, let us lay aside every weight, and the sin which so easily ensnares us" (Hebrews 12:1). We need to make a determined decision that we will not allow into our lives anything that will keep us from becoming the people God wants us to be.

There are many people in this life who have built their own barrier to progress. They have built their own barrier to prosperity. They have built their own barrier to love, because they refuse to surrender what is poisoning their life. As a result, they go through life wanting to blame somebody. Sometimes they just want to blame society—"Well, it's the fault of this country I live in," or, "It's because of these people." All that blame doesn't get them anything but frustration, anxiety, anger, and more unforgiveness.

As we will discuss in this study, we can't make unforgiveness "fit" anywhere in our lives as believers in Christ. We can never come to the point where we just stop forgiving because God's Word tells us there is no point where we can stop forgiving. Furthermore, if we stop forgiving, we will suffer the consequences—we will become one of these bitter and resentful people I've just mentioned. You say, "But suppose they continue on in their hurtful behavior?" What do we do? We must continue on forgiving. Otherwise, we suffer the consequences.

7. What are some of the by-products of unforgiveness that you have seen in others' lives?

8. "Let us lay aside every weight . . . and let us run with endurance the race that is set before us" (Hebrews 12:1). How do bitterness and unforgiveness get in the way of us running the "race" that God has set before us with endurance?

The Fruit of Unforgiveness

The author of the book of Hebrews provides us with a great overview of what happens when a person refuses to be forgiving:

> Pursue peace with all people, and holiness, without which no one will see the Lord: looking carefully lest anyone fall short of the grace of God; lest any root of bitterness springing up cause trouble, and by this many become defiled; lest there be any fornicator or profane person like Esau, who for one morsel of food sold his birthright. For you know that afterward, when he wanted to inherit the blessing, he was rejected, for he found no place for repentance, though he sought it diligently with tears (Hebrews 12:14–17).

In the Greek, the word translated as *looking* in verse 15 means, "concentrate on this, don't overlook this, make it your business."

To do what? To see that no root of bitterness springs up in our lives that would cause trouble. The author says, "by this many become defiled," which simply means we can't keep bitterness to ourselves.

And bitterness is a choice that each of make. If somebody hurts us, we have a choice to be bitter, resentful, hostile, angry, and to retaliate against that person. It's a choice we make. If we choose to sow those seeds, we will reap a harvest of the fruits of bitterness. All kinds of negative things grow up out of bitterness. All of them are negative in their effects upon us.

Take for example a glass of crystal-clear water. It doesn't take but one drop of dark blue ink to turn the whole thing blue. The whole glass is affected by it. Bitterness is a destructive attitude, and it's an attitude that *overflows*. Bitter people cannot keep it to themselves.

You say, "Well, I'm a private kind of person. Nobody knows that I'm bitter." Oh yes, they do. You can't keep it to yourself, because that's the nature of it. Bitterness is a destroyer, and it's nature is to destroy the people around you. People lose their jobs because their unforgiving and bitter spirit. They lose their family because of their bitterness. They lose close relationships with their children because those children can't stand that kind of bitterness and mistreatment from their parents. There is a price to pay for an unforgiving spirit.

Sadly, many people have believed the devil's lie that they can keep bitterness and unforgiveness to themselves and it won't hurt them or anyone else. "Look at you. You're just fine. You're doing well." Well, you cannot live long with bitterness before it begins to show up in a fashion that you don't want. Bitterness yields a bitter harvest. As Paul states, "Now the works of the flesh are evident, which are: adultery, fornication, uncleanness, lewdness, idolatry, sorcery, hatred, contentions, jealousies, outbursts of wrath, selfish ambitions, dissensions, heresies, envy, murders, drunkenness, revelries, and the like" (Galatians 5:19–21).

But forgiveness brings with it a harvest of the fruit of the Spirit: "love, joy, peace, longsuffering, kindness, goodness, faithfulness, gentleness, self-control" (verses 22–23). Therefore, in the following lessons, we will explore what it means to be forgiven and what we need to do to experience God's complete forgiveness in our lives.

9. "Do not be deceived, God is not mocked; for whatever a man sows, that he will also reap" (Galatians 6:7). How does this verse apply to sowing seeds of bitterness? How does it apply to sowing seeds of love and forgiveness?

10. "In Him we have redemption through His blood, the forgiveness of sins, according to the riches of His grace" (Ephesians 1:7). From where does all forgiveness originate? How can you tap into this "source"?

TODAY AND TOMORROW

Today: Sin does matter, but forgiveness is the only solution to sin's damages.

Tomorrow: I will ask the Lord to show me areas where I need forgiveness and where I need to forgive.

Closing Prayer

Lord Jesus, thank You for loving us. Thank You for giving Your life on the cross so we could receive the forgiveness of sins. Today, we pray the Holy Spirit would surface in our hearts and minds and root out any seeds of unforgiveness that are within us—even seeds we do not realize that we have planted. We want to produce a harvest of Your fruit of gentleness, kindness, and love and not the fruit that our bitterness will inevitably yield. Please begin the healing process of restoration and reconciliation within us. We pray in Jesus' name and for His sake. Amen.

Notes and Prayer Requests

Use this space to write any key points, questions, or prayer requests from this week's study.

LESSON 2

Can Everybody Be Forgiven?

IN THIS LESSON

Learning: What is "the unpardonable sin"?

Growing: How can I be assured of my forgiveness?

Do you ever ask yourself any of these questions: "Have I committed the unpardonable sin? Can I ever be free of the weight of this guilt? Will God forgive every sin?" If so, I have good news for you today! Your loving heavenly Father will forgive you of your sin. You can be released today from all your sin if you will do what God says to do.

The apostle Paul once dealt with an instance of sexual immorality in the Corinthian church. It was a case of incest in which a man had taken his father's wife. The woman was not his mother, but the law of God condemns the act as a vile abomination.

Against that backdrop, Paul wrote, "Do you not know that the unrighteous will not inherit the kingdom of God? Do not be deceived. Neither fornicators, nor idolaters, nor adulterers, nor homosexuals, nor sodomites, nor thieves, nor covetous, nor drunkards, nor revilers, nor extortioners will inherit the kingdom of God. And such were some of you. But you were washed, but you were sanctified, but you were justified in the name of the Lord Jesus and by the Spirit of our God" (1 Corinthians 6:9–11).

The Nature of Sin

This passage Paul wrote to the Corinthian believers holds three great messages for us today. *First, it tells us that sin is sin.* God doesn't differentiate between one type of sin and another. Most of us wouldn't think of revilers (slanderers) as being in the same category as thieves, but God doesn't have categories of sin. Sin is sin.

Later in the same chapter, Paul made a distinction between the sin of sexual immorality and other sins, teaching that "every sin that a man does is outside the body, but he who commits sexual immorality sins against his own body" (verse 18). But this is a differentiation of sin according to the effects of certain sinful behaviors, not the nature of sin itself.

Second, Paul's words to the Corinthians tells us that sin is a lifestyle, a mindset, and a state of being. Paul was not condemning one specific act or behavior among the people in the church; rather, he was stating that sin had been the identity of the Corinthians in the past. Sin had been their all-consuming character. For example, he didn't say, "Some of you have taken things that weren't yours." Paul called them former *thieves*—people who had stolen as a way of life. He didn't say, "Some of you had one too many drinks on occasion." He said some in the Corinthian church were *drunkards.*

Now, before you start thinking, "Well, I haven't been any of the things on Paul's list," let me advise you this is not a definitive list.

Paul wasn't trying to list all types of sinners. Rather, he was giving examples of the sinful state to point out the same truth he shared with the Roman believers: "All have sinned and fall short of the glory of God" (Romans 3:23). Every person, before receiving a new identity in Christ Jesus, has had the identity of a sinner.

Some people look back over their lives and conclude, "I've never done anything very bad. I'm a pretty good person and always have been." Sometimes they conclude, "What is there that God needs to forgive?" They have missed the entire point about sin and forgiveness. They have been taught a wrong perspective on life. This is the perspective the Romans apparently had, for Paul spent much of his letter to them teaching that they were born with a sin nature. Sin isn't something that you *do*. Being sinful is something that you *are* from birth.

Third, this passage tells us that all types of sin can be forgiven. Paul said, "And such *were* some of you" (verse 11, emphasis added). Then Paul reminded them they were no longer who they once were but had been washed, sanctified, and justified in the name of the Lord Jesus and by the Spirit of God. The Corinthians found a new life—a new identity—in Christ Jesus!

Note the words that Paul used:

- *Washed:* Paul spoke of a cleansing of the spirit. So did the psalmist when he wrote these words: "Purge me with hyssop, and I shall be clean; wash me, and I shall be whiter than snow" (Psalm 51:7).

- *Sanctified:* Something that is sanctified is dedicated to God, set aside for holy uses. In Old Testament times, blood from sacrificed animals was applied to certain vessels in the tabernacle to make them holy for God's use. In Hebrews 13:12, we read, "Therefore Jesus also, that He might sanctify the people with His own blood, suffered." When God forgives us, He sets us aside—apart from the world of unredeemed, unregenerate, unforgiven humankind—and considers us to be solely for His purposes and fellowship.

- *Justified:* When we justify something, we line it up—for example, we justify the margins on a page or we justify our legal arguments against the law of the land. When we are justified in our actions, we are vindicated. In forgiveness, God lines us up against the truth of what Jesus did on the cross and declares us to be righteous just because we are lined up with Jesus. We aren't righteous in ourselves, but the shed blood of Jesus justifies us before God.

Nothing is beyond God's forgiveness. No sin is too great, or too awful, or too prolific for God to forgive. No person is so deep in sin, or so ingrained in a lifestyle, or so steeped in evil, that he or she cannot be saved.

1. "But you were washed, but you were sanctified, but you were justified in the name of the Lord Jesus and by the Spirit of our God" (1 Corinthians 6:11). In your own words, how would you define the terms *washed, sanctified,* and *justified*?

2. Use the table below to identify who you were before you received Jesus as Savior and who you are now.

I once was . . .	But now I am . . .

An Alarm System

Previously, I defined *forgiveness* as "the act of setting someone free." *Sin*, by contrast, is "the state of being in bondage—in need of being set free." The psalmist describes this state in Psalm 51 as the result of transgressions, iniquity, sin, and evil.

We do what we do because we are sinners. Our sinful actions seal the fact we are sinners. Our being and doing are cyclical. We may not always admit to being sinners, but deep inside we recognize we are sinners and we have an awareness we have sinned or are sinning. Sinners know at some level they are sinning. Sin involves the will and affects the memory—we remember our sins. The psalmist is very open about this: "For I acknowledge my transgressions, and my sin is always before me" (Psalm 51:3).

How do we know we are sinners or we have sinned? God built into us an alarm system called the *conscience.* It sounds each time we do something (or are about to do something) we know is wrong. If we ignore the alarm system, our sensitivity to evil becomes dull, and eventually we stop hearing it. A healthy conscience is something to cherish and to nurture.

The flaw in the conscience, however, is that it is based on human understanding of what is right and wrong. The difference between right and wrong is something we learn. Unfortunately, some people are taught that right is wrong and wrong is right. They make decisions and behave in ways that are sinful with little remorse—that is, until they are confronted with the truth.

The conscience always is pricked to some degree in the presence of the pure expression of the gospel of our Lord Jesus Christ. Jesus Christ is "the way, the truth, and the life" (John 14:6). He stands in sharp contrast to all that leads to destruction. He opposes all that is a lie or that contributes to death. In the presence of the gospel, even the most warped conscience is confronted with God's absolutes.

Believers in Christ actually have a *dual* alarm system. They have the natural conscience given to every person, and they also have the Holy Spirit indwelling them. The Holy Spirit provides counsel that they are acting, or are about to act, in a way contrary to God's desire. The Holy Spirit always points a believer toward Jesus and the fullness of the Word of God. Jesus called the Holy Spirit the "Spirit of truth," our divine counselor (see John 15:26).

The Holy Spirit will never quit speaking to you once you have received Him into your life. Your spiritual ears may become dull, but you can never completely silence the Holy Spirit. If you don't feel the Holy Spirit pricking your heart from time to time, you may need to ask, "Am I really saved? Have I really received forgiveness from God for my sinful state?" Listen to your conscience and to the Holy Spirit today. He will tell you whether you are in need of forgiveness.

3. "Your ears shall hear a word behind you, saying, 'This is the way, walk in it,' whenever you turn to the right hand or whenever you turn to the left" (Isaiah 30:21). How does this passage describe a godly conscience? When have you heard this voice in your life?

4. "I will pray the Father, and He will give you another Helper, that He may abide with you forever—the Spirit of truth, whom the world cannot receive, because it neither sees Him nor knows Him; but you know Him, for He dwells with you and will be in you" (John 14:16–17). What names and qualities of the Holy Spirit are found in these verses?

5. What does the Holy Spirit do? What are we expected to do?

What About the Unpardonable Sin?

Let's take a close look at the passage of Scripture that describes the unpardonable sin. In Matthew 12, Jesus and His disciples pluck and eat some heads of grain as they pass through a field. Then, while in a synagogue, He heals a man with a withered hand. Jesus does these things on the Sabbath, and the Pharisees speak out against Him and begin to plot to destroy Him (see verses 1–13). Jesus knows what they are planning.

Then Jesus heals a person who is demon-possessed and cannot see or speak. There can be no doubt this man has been healed in a powerful way. But the Pharisees, intent solely on destroying any credibility that Jesus might have with the people, insist He has healed by the power of Beelzebub, the ruler of the demons. Jesus replies, "Every kingdom divided against itself is brought to desolation" (verse 25). In other words, Satan isn't going to empower or inspire anybody to do something that is good. Satan would be setting up his own downfall.

The Pharisees are claiming God would not empower someone like Jesus to do good on the Sabbath. They are saying, in essence, "God is content to let certain people suffer on the Sabbath, but the ruler of the demons, Beelzebub, is willing to see such people helped." What a complete perversion of the truth about God's nature and also about the devil's nature!

Jesus states, "He who is not with Me is against Me, and he who does not gather with Me scatters abroad" (verse 30). Then He says these words, which are considered the definition of the unpardonable sin: "Therefore I say to you, every sin and blasphemy will be forgiven men, but the blasphemy against the Spirit will not be forgiven men. Anyone who speaks a word against the Son of Man, it will be forgiven him; but whoever speaks against the Holy Spirit, it will not be forgiven him, either in this age or in the age to come" (verses 31–32).

Jesus is saying, "You can say what you will about Me, but don't speak such perversion about the Spirit of God. When you blaspheme against God in that way, you are saying God does not desire to forgive and deliver people. As long as you believe that and teach that to others, you won't be able to experience His forgiveness and deliverance. If you don't believe God wants to forgive people and restore them to wholeness, then you will never be open to the sacrifice that I will make on the cross of Calvary."

These words of Jesus were to the Pharisees—a group of people who had put themselves into sharp conflict with Him and were plotting His destruction. He was speaking to them before His death on the cross and before His resurrection. He spoke these words as a warning to the Pharisees to let them know He knew the intent of their hearts and meaning of their claims.

Jesus says immediately after this warning, "Either make the tree good and its fruit good, or else make the tree bad and its fruit bad; for a tree is known by its fruit. Brood of vipers! How can you, being evil, speak good things?" (verses 33–34). Jesus is saying, "Either make Me good and of a good God, or make Me bad and call God bad. Judge what I do. Is it good or bad? I'm willing to do that regarding you. I call you a brood of snakes. And since you are evil, I say plainly there is no way that anything you say can be good."

The unpardonable sin is the sin of the Pharisees, committed before the cross. It is not a sin you need to be concerned about today.

If you have any concern about having committed the unpardonable sin—any concern you might not be right with God, even though you hope and desire to be right with God—you have not committed the unpardonable sin!

Let me point out two other facts based on God's Word. *First, there is no exception clause in any of the Scriptures that offer salvation.* John 3:16 does *not* say, "For God so loved the world—except those who have committed a certain type of sin—that He gave His only begotten Son, that whoever—except those who are sinners of a particular brand—should not perish but have everlasting life." No! God's call to salvation is a call to all sinners.

Second, there is no warning in the Gospels or the Epistles about an unpardonable sin. Paul, Peter, John, and the other writers of the New Testament did not say to us, "Watch out for this one sin. God can forgive all sins but that one." No! There is no sin that is unforgivable on this side of the grave.

The sin that grieves the Holy Spirit and can quench the work of the Spirit in your life is a refusal to receive the forgiveness that God freely offers to you. You can refuse God's offer of forgiveness to the point you have a hardened heart. You can become calcified to the gospel over time. And that creates an *unpardonable state.*

The Lord God will not reach beyond the boundaries of your own free will and save you against your will! You can die in an unpardonable state, but it won't be because you have committed an unpardonable sin. As I stated above, no sin is unforgivable on this side of death. It is equally true that no sin can be forgiven on the other side of the grave.

The only thing that can keep you from being forgiven is the refusal to *accept and receive* what Jesus Christ has done for you on the cross. Refusing to accept the forgiveness made available by the death of Christ brings about everlasting death. Accepting what Jesus did on the cross—believing in Him as Savior—brings about everlasting life.

6. "If we say that we have no sin, we deceive ourselves, and the truth is not in us. If we confess our sins, He is faithful and just to forgive us our sins and to cleanse us from all unrighteousness" (1 John 1:8–9). What is required to receive forgiveness of sins?

7. What is the only condition listed in Scripture where a person does *not* receive forgiveness?

Forgiveness Must Only Be Received

Have you made a decision to accept and receive Jesus as your personal Savior? To *accept* and *receive*—that is all that is required for you to be forgiven by God, regardless of the nature, magnitude, or deep entrenchment of your sins.

To *accept* is to believe with your mind what the Bible says about Jesus and His death on the cross—that Jesus died for your sins and rose to give you new life in Him. To *receive* is to say, "I don't merely accept what Jesus did on the cross as a fact of history, but I also accept His sacrificial death for me personally—the sacrifice that was made for my sins. I invite the Holy Spirit to indwell me, to cleanse me of all my past sin, and to make me a new person in God's eyes. I receive the work of the Holy Spirit in me that gives me a completely restored relationship with my heavenly Father."

God desires to forgive you today. Have you taken Him up on His offer? If not, will you accept and receive Jesus Christ today? Will you receive God's forgiveness?

8. "Not by works of righteousness which we have done, but according to His mercy He saved us, through the washing of regeneration and renewing of the Holy Spirit" (Titus 3:5). What are "works of righteousness"? Why can such things never wash away sin?

9. How would you describe the "washing of regeneration"? What is involved in that process?

10. What is *our* part in regeneration and renewing? What is the Holy Spirit's part?

TODAY AND TOMORROW

Today: The only unpardonable sin is rejecting Jesus' free offer of salvation.

Tomorrow: I will yield myself to the Holy Spirit, confessing my sins quickly.

CLOSING PRAYER

Father, we pray You would teach us to deal with sin so we never excuse it or rationalize it but to continuously recognize the awesome price that Jesus paid for our forgiveness. Thank You for the inner alarm system—our conscience—that You have placed within each of us to convict us when we sin. Help us to recognize that You have promised to forgive all our sins when we choose to face them, confess them to You, and receive Your gift of forgiveness. Teach us how to live in the freedom and the liberty that is ours through the shed blood Jesus Christ. We thank You that we are indeed living in the ever-cleansing of that precious blood so we are not guilty before You but accepted, loved, and cherished as Your children. Amen.

Notes and Prayer Requests

Use this space to write any key points, questions, or prayer requests from this week's study.

LESSON 3

THE FOUNDATION FOR OUR FORGIVENESS

IN THIS LESSON

Learning: If sin is so awful, why does God forgive it?

Growing: What is my role in attaining forgiveness?

Why does God forgive people? Many people think God *has* to forgive people for one reason or another. But the truth is that God doesn't *have* to do anything! In the Bible, we read how Job came to this conclusion at the end of his long period of adversity when he declared, "I know that You can do *everything*, and that no purpose of Yours can be withheld from You. . . . I have uttered what I did not understand, things too wonderful for me, which I did not know" (Job 42:2–3, emphasis added). Contrary to some people's ideas, God certainly doesn't forgive for any of the following reasons.

Wrong Understandings of God's Forgiveness

God doesn't forgive us because we are "good people." We all know we *aren't* good. Jesus said, "No one is good but One, that is, God" (Matthew 19:17). We live in a fallen world and are born in a fallen state. As the apostle Paul wrote:

> Therefore, just as through one man sin entered the world, and death through sin, and thus death spread to all men, because all sinned. . . . Nevertheless death reigned from Adam to Moses, even over those who had not sinned according to the likeness of the transgression of Adam, who is a type of Him who was to come (Romans 5:12, 14).

Like it or not, we are Adam's heirs. We are born in a sinful state, separated from God, and in need of God's forgiveness and reconciliation.

God doesn't forgive us because we promise never to sin again. In all probability, we *will* sin again . . . and God knows it, even if we won't admit it to ourselves.

God doesn't forgive us because we go to church or give money to worthy causes. Our works, as noble as they may be, have nothing to do with our salvation. Paul states this clearly in Ephesians 2:8–9: "For by grace you have been saved through faith, and that not of yourselves; it is the gift of God, not of works, lest anyone should boast."

God doesn't forgive us because He is having a good day and just feels kindly toward us. God is not capricious, bestowing forgiveness on us one day and withholding it from us on the next. God's nature doesn't change, He isn't ruled by whim, and He doesn't operate according to an emotional barometer. When things go well, some people comment, "I think that God was smiling on me today." The fact is that God is *always* smiling on us.

God doesn't forgive us because we ask Him to forgive us. God does forgive us *when* we ask Him, but He doesn't forgive us *because* we ask Him. If so, it would imply God is in a state of unforgiveness toward us until we ask—which simply isn't the case. God is always extending an offer of forgiveness to us. Our plea for forgiveness doesn't move God to action. He has already moved toward us—all the way from heaven right to the place where we live in our sin—and He is waiting for us to turn to Him and receive the forgiveness He offers.

God doesn't forgive us because He is a good God and would never send anybody to hell. This is one of the foremost heresies of our time. I hear it often: "God is a good God, and He would never condemn a person to an eternity without Him." This isn't what the Bible teaches.

For instance, we find these words immediately following John 3:16: "For God did not send His Son into the world to condemn the world, but that the world through Him might be saved. He who believes in Him is not condemned; but he who does not believe is condemned already, because he has not believed in the name of the only begotten Son of God. And this is the condemnation, that the light has come into the world, and men loved darkness rather than light, because their deeds were evil" (verses 17–19).

Our actions condemn us. God doesn't desire any should perish, but He will not override our will. If we choose to reject God's offer of forgiveness, we have chosen our eternal destiny without God.

1. "All have sinned and fall short of the glory of God" (Romans 3:23). Why can't the fact that you may be a "good person" save you from God's judgment against sin?

2. "But when the kindness and the love of God our Savior toward man appeared, not by works of righteousness which we have done, but according to His mercy He saved us, through the washing of regeneration and renewing of the Holy Spirit" (Titus 3:4–5). According to these verses, why can't your good works save you?

3. "And this is the condemnation, that the light has come into the world, and men loved darkness rather than light, because their deeds were evil" (John 3:19). What prevents people from accepting God's gift of salvation? What is the result of rejecting Jesus?

God's Motivation to Forgive

The motivation for God's forgiveness lies totally within God Himself. He forgives us because He wants to forgive. God forgives out of His unconditional and eternal love. John tells us that God's very nature is love and that forgiveness flows from His nature: "He who does not love does not know God, for God is love. In this the love of God was manifested toward us, that God has sent His only begotten Son into the world, that we might live through Him. In this is love, not that we loved God, but that He loved us and sent His Son to be the propitiation for our sins" (1 John 4:8–10). We are forgiven simply because it is God's *will* to forgive.

4. "But God, who is rich in mercy, because of His great love with which He loved us, even when we were dead in trespasses, made us alive together with Christ (by grace you have been saved)" (Ephesians 2:4–5). According to these verses, why does God forgive?

5. According to these verses, what happens when you receive Christ as your Savior?

God Sets the Rules for Forgiveness

Forgiveness is totally at God's initiative and subject to His will alone. Given this, we must ask, "Has God established any rules or protocol for forgiveness?" He certainly has.

We must recognize that God is holy, which means He is separate from humankind in nature. God has no capacity for sin, and He cannot have fellowship with sin. God is totally pure, righteous, and without fault. He cannot coexist where sin is present.

Light and dark do not exist simultaneously. In a similar manner, our sin cannot exist in God's presence. God obliterates sin just as light obliterates darkness, and in this we find a picture of our vulnerability before God when we are filled with sin. We are subject to being consumed by Him as darkness is consumed by light, having the innermost being vaporized by His fire of righteousness. In a word, we are subject to death.

God made a provision, however, for us to be cleansed of sin so we might have fellowship with Him—and that provision was in the form of a blood sacrifice. "But I don't like this idea of blood," you may say. The idea of blood sacrifice was not our idea—it was God's. It is not within our prerogative to choose another means for reconciliation with God. God sets the rules in this matter, and God established the blood sacrifice as a means of reconciling us to Him.

There is no forgiveness without blood sacrifice. This theme is in the Bible from cover to cover. When Cain and Abel made sacrificial offerings to God, the offering that God accepted was the blood sacrifice of a lamb (see Genesis 4:2–5.) The sacrifices atoned for sin under the law of Moses were blood sacrifices. In like manner, the blood of Jesus shed on the cross is the *sacrificial, substitutionary, all-sufficient atonement* for our sins. Each of the words in the previous sentence is important to our understanding of the forgiveness made available to us through the death of Jesus Christ.

First, the blood Jesus shed was sacrificial. Jesus wasn't put to death by the Romans or the Jewish leaders. On the contrary, He appeared in history to "put away sin by the sacrifice of Himself" (Hebrews 9:26). Jesus gave His life, as an act of His will conforming to the Father's will, as the "Lamb slain from the foundation of the world" (Revelation 13:8).

Second, the blood Jesus shed was substitutionary. Jesus took your place on the cross. He died in your place and in my place, and in the place of everyone you know. The penalty for sin is death—and we are all sinners. Unless One who was pure and righteous took our place and suffered the penalty for our sin, we would have to bear that penalty ourselves. The apostle Paul explained this in Romans 3:10–18 by citing several verses from the Old Testament:

> There is none righteous, no, not one; there is none who understands; there is none who seeks after God. They have all turned aside; they have together become unprofitable; there is none who does good, no, not one. Their throat is an open tomb; with their tongues they have practiced deceit; the poison of asps is under their lips; whose mouth is full of cursing and bitterness. Their feet are swift to shed blood; destruction and misery are in their ways; and the way of peace they have not known. There is no fear of God before their eyes.

Third, the blood Jesus shed was all-sufficient. The work that Jesus did was definitive. We no longer need to offer blood sacrifices in acknowledgment of our sin. We only need to have faith in Jesus Christ and to accept what He has done on our behalf. The writer of Hebrews says that God took away the first means of blood sacrifice so that He might establish the second means: the sacrifice of Jesus. The sacrifice of Jesus was the only one necessary. The phrase the writer uses is a powerful one: "once for all" (Hebrews 10:10).

Fourth, the blood Jesus shed provided atonement for our sins. The word *atonement* means "reconciliation"—you can think of it as "at-one-ment." Jesus' death on the cross made it possible for the gap to be bridged between God and His fallen creation. In Romans 5:1, Paul speaks of atonement in terms of peace: "Therefore, having been justified by faith, we have peace with God through our Lord Jesus Christ." What Jesus did on the cross, He never needs to do again, and neither does anyone else ever have to suffer and die as He did.

Jesus is the *sacrificial, substitutionary, all-sufficient atonement.*

6. "For the death that He died, He died to sin once for all; but the life that He lives, He lives to God. Likewise you also, reckon yourselves to be dead indeed to sin, but alive to God in Christ Jesus our Lord" (Romans 6:10–11). What does it mean to be "dead to sin"? How do we balance this statement from Paul with the fact that Christians still commit sin?

7. Why does Paul tell us to "reckon ourselves" (or think of ourselves) as being dead to sin? What does our thinking have to do with the process?

Jesus: Example or Sacrifice?

Some people believe Jesus came to be our example of how to live a good life. To be sure, Jesus is our example of righteousness. We are to grow up into His nature and become like Him. But that isn't the reason Jesus came into this world. Jesus came to *die*. His purpose was to be the sacrificial, substitutionary, all-sufficient atonement. If Jesus didn't come for this reason, then why did He die? What purpose would His death have if not for forgiveness?

Jesus could have spared His own life. His power to calm a raging sea, heal, and deliver is evidence of His ability to summon the forces of heaven on His behalf. His quick thinking and speaking in outwitting the scribes and Pharisees are evidence that He could have argued His case favorably before Pilate. If Jesus had insisted on His natural human will in the matter, He could have walked away from Gethsemane, walked away from Jerusalem, and walked away from the cross long before His arrest in the Garden. But He submitted His will to that of His heavenly Father, saying, "Not as I will, but as You will" (Matthew 26:39).

If Jesus didn't come to die, there is no purpose in the cross or the resurrection that followed. Some say Jesus was sacrificed as a ransom to buy off the devil. But the Bible offers no evidence for that. Others say Jesus died a holy, righteous man as a bitter example to us that sin is awful and destructive—to the point that we kill the best and the brightest. But such reasoning violates every principle of salvation, softens the death consequence of sin, and belittles the holiness of God. It is an idea deeply rooted in humanistic religion.

Again and again in the New Testament we are confronted with the message: *Christ died for us.* Jesus came so that we might transfer our guilt to Him and accept, by faith, that He is the guiltless One who has received our sin and taken it on Himself. If you are looking for forgiveness on the basis of your pleas, promises, and performance, you will remain in sin and guilt. If you accept His sacrifice on your behalf, you will receive the fullness of God's life-giving Spirit.

8. On the night of Jesus' arrest in the Garden of Gethsemane, He said to His disciples, "Do you think that I cannot now pray to My Father, and He will provide Me with more than twelve legions of angels?" (Matthew 26:53). What does this say about Jesus' ability to save His own life?

9. "My little children, these things I write to you, so that you may not sin. And if anyone sins, we have an Advocate with the Father, Jesus Christ the righteous" (1 John 2:1). Why does John say that he is writing his words "so that you may not sin," and then immediately speak about times when we do sin?

10. What is an "advocate"? What sort of advocate is Jesus?

TODAY AND TOMORROW

Today: God has forgiven me because He wanted to do so—it's that simple.

Tomorrow: I will reflect on what my free salvation cost God.

Closing Prayer

Lord Jesus, thank You for being our example of righteousness. But even more, thank You for coming into this world for the purpose of dying on the cross for our sins. Thank You that through Your atoning death we can receive forgiveness and freedom from our sins. We are grateful today for the privilege of walking in Your spirit of forgiveness. We acknowledge that we do not have to carry all the luggage of an unforgiving spirit—and all the terrible weight of the pressure, tension, and strife that it brings. We know all the things that come with an unforgiving spirit of hostility: resentment, bitterness, ill will, and a critical spirit. We desire today, Lord, to accept Your offer that we can be free of these things—because You have made us free. Amen.

Notes and Prayer Requests

Use this space to write any key points, questions, or prayer requests from this week's study.

LESSON 4

A Matter of Life and Death

IN THIS LESSON

Learning: What exactly is sin?

Growing: Why do I need forgiveness in the first place?

Forgiveness is a matter of life and death—eternal life and death. In truth, there is nothing more important than receiving God's forgiveness and being reconciled to Him. In this lesson, we will build on the concepts we discussed previously about sin and forgiveness. I want to take you to a greater understanding of what the Bible teaches about sin, guilt, and our need for a Savior.

You may be a Christian and therefore believe you don't need to know anything more about sin and guilt. Well, as a Christian, you should be talking to people who are sinners about their need for forgiveness. This lesson can give you some insights into what to say about sin and forgiveness and how to encourage a person to accept Christ as Savior.

But let's begin by recognizing several facts about genuine guilt versus false guilt. *Genuine guilt* is the way we feel when we have sinned. It is the normal response to sinful behavior. Sin causes guilt . . . but not all guilt comes from sin.

Sometimes, the guilt we feel is *false guilt*. Consider, for example, a young woman who is a victim of incest or rape. She may struggle for years with a sense of guilt because she has been a party to a sin. But she was neither the initiator of nor a willing participant in that sin. She is a victim of someone else's sin. The guilt that she feels is false guilt. It is false because, from God's perspective, there is no accountability placed on her for what happened. Genuine guilt is associated with willful sin, not sin that is against one's will.

1. When have you deliberately done something you knew was wrong? Did you feel guilty?

2. When have you been a participant in a sin against your will? Have you felt guilty?

An Accountability Ladder Involving the Will

Genuine guilt arises when we willfully act in a way that we know is contrary to God's law. An accountability ladder involving the will looks something like this:

forgiveness
sin and guilt
knowledge
moral conscience

Forgiveness presupposes sin and its attendant guilt. In other words, if you feel no guilt of sin, you feel no need for forgiveness. Guilt presupposes knowledge. If you don't know you have sinned, you don't feel guilty. Knowledge presupposes a moral conscience—that you have the capacity for determining right from wrong. If you don't have a moral conscience, then you don't know whether you are doing wrong. If you are unable to determine right from wrong—as is the case with some mental disorders—then God does not hold you accountable for your actions.

In this entire chain of presuppositions is the concept of the *will*. Put the process in reverse: If you have the capacity to know right from wrong, and if you know something is wrong but you choose to do it anyway, you will feel guilty and have a need for forgiveness. You have acted out of your will to do something that you know not to do. You have willfully acted in a way that is wrong and you are accountable for your actions.

You may say, "Are you telling me that if I don't know that something is wrong, I'm not accountable for that sin?" That is exactly what I'm saying. But hear me carefully when I say very few people fall into that category. Most of us know what to do. Most of us know what not to do. And most of us choose, at some points in our lives, to do what we know not to do. This is true for all people. Human beings around the world have an intuitive sense of what is right and wrong, and they know when they are choosing wrong.

Consider a three-year-old girl who is told, "Don't touch Mommy's special vase." The child is brought into the living room and instructed, "In this room, I want you to look at things but not touch them." The child may even be shown the vase and be allowed to touch it under careful supervision while her mother says, "This is the vase I don't want you to touch, except when I am with you and we are touching it just as we are touching it right now."

The mother asks the child, "Do you understand what I am telling you?" The child nods yes and may even say, "I won't touch your vase, Mommy." The next hour, what does Mommy hear from the living room? The crash of her favorite vase.

Now, nobody had to teach that little girl to disobey. We teach our children to obey, but they are born with the ability to disobey. In the same way, even when we know we aren't to do certain things because God has commanded us not to do them, we sometimes still choose to do those things. As Paul wrote, "The carnal mind is enmity against God; for it is not subject to the law of God, nor indeed can be" (Romans 8:7). We are born with a rebellious nature, and we are accountable for our deeds performed in rebellion against God's commandments.

Again, guilt is genuine guilt when it is the byproduct of our willful sin. Guilt is false guilt when it is the by-product of another person's willful sin. So, what should people do if they discover they have been carrying a load of false guilt? They should come before their heavenly Father and say, "I confess that I have been carrying a burden that isn't mine. I give this burden of guilt to You today, Lord Jesus. I turn it over to You completely and ask You to carry it. I receive Your forgiveness, and by my faith, I accept the fact that I am free of this guilt and any aspect of sin associated with it. In Jesus' name, amen!"

3. "For to be carnally minded is death, but to be spiritually minded is life and peace. Because the carnal mind is enmity against God; for it is not subject to the law of God, nor indeed can be" (Romans 8:6–7). What does it mean to be "carnally minded"? What does it mean to be "spiritually minded"?

4. What real-life examples can you provide of being carnally minded? How do those actions display opposition to God?

A Definition of Sin

Some people define *sin* as "missing the mark"—just as an arrow misses a bull's-eye on a target. God's commandments are the target, and we miss God's ideal when we sin. Others define *sin* as "falling short" of God's perfect will. God's desire is that we live in wholeness and follow Him explicitly in all His commandments and directives. We fail to do so in our imperfection, and that is sin. Still others define *sin* as "trespassing." God has areas of behavior that He designates off-limits to us, and we trespass into those territories and are subject to penalty. We have sinned against God and others.

My personal favorite definition of sin comes from Jeremiah 2:13:

> For My people have committed two evils:
> They have forsaken Me, the fountain of living waters,
> And hewn themselves cisterns—broken cisterns that can
> hold no water.

Cisterns are wells that are dug into the earth, usually into solid rock, with the intention of holding water. God is painting a fascinating picture in these words of the prophet. He is saying, "You have rejected Me as a fountain of living water for your life." A fountain is an artesian spring—one that bubbles up from the earth with an unending supply of fresh, pure water. A fountain gives water that is free for the taking.

Jesus once encountered a Samaritan woman by the well of Sychar, and in the course of His conversation with her, He said of Himself, "If you knew the gift of God, and who it is who says to you, 'Give Me a drink,' you would have asked Him, and He would have given you living water" (John 4:10). Jesus was painting this same word picture about Himself—He has life to give that is eternal and is freely offered. His forgiveness is a fountain from which we can draw in an unending fashion. His forgiveness is free for the asking.

"But," God says, "instead of choosing My living water, you chose to build cisterns." To build is an act of the will. The cistern builders rejected the artesian spring for a well of their own making. The Lord noted with sadness but with certainty, "It is a broken well." There was a crack in the cistern, which meant that it wouldn't hold the water. "Everything that you do to achieve your own forgiveness is futile," God is saying. "You can dig and dig, you can make cistern after cistern, you can strive and struggle all you want, and it will never bring you forgiveness."

The only forgiveness we can ever experience is God's forgiveness, granted God's way. Any time we attempt to accomplish anything by means other than God's means, we are setting ourselves up for eventual failure—we are building a broken cistern. If we want to be our own savior rather than accept the Savior whom God has provided, we will fail in our attempt.

5. Recall, in detail, one time when you willfully chose your way over what you knew to be God's way. What was the result?

6. "For My people have committed two evils: They have forsaken Me, the fountain of living waters, And hewn themselves cisterns—broken cisterns that can hold no water" (Jeremiah 2:13). Why does God list these sins separately? In your own words, what are these sins: forsaking God's water, and building your own cistern?

A Willful Choice Against God

Ultimately, people's willful choices against God can form a pattern that leads to eternal death. God doesn't send people to hell—people choose to go there.

People choose to trample on the blood of Jesus. They choose to walk nonchalantly past the cross. They choose to avoid the empty tomb. They choose to ignore the songs of redemption they have heard. They choose to harden their hearts to the prayers of others on their behalf. They choose to turn a deaf ear to sermons that speak of salvation and to the witness of Christ's love from friends and strangers. They choose to ignore and repress the countless promptings of the Holy Spirit tugging at their hearts. They choose to rebel.

People really have to *work* to refuse God's gift of forgiveness—but some do. They refuse to give up their pride and to submit to doing things God's way. They refuse to drink from the fountain of His living water freely made available to them. They strive instead to build cisterns—cisterns that inevitably will break and fail to satisfy the deep thirst of the soul.

7. "Behold, I set before you today a blessing and a curse: the blessing, if you obey the commandments of the LORD your God which I command you today; and the curse, if you do not obey the commandments of the LORD your God, but turn aside from the way which I command you today" (Deuteronomy 11:26-28). What do these words from Moses say about the *choice* that each person has been given in regard to God?

8. What are some reasons you have heard as to why people refuse God's free gift of salvation? What fears do they have if they choose to submit to God?

Forgiveness Is a Gift

Throughout the New Testament, forgiveness is pictured as a gift of God. Paul tells us, "The wages of sin is death, but the gift of God is eternal life in Christ Jesus" (Romans 6:23). A gift is free to you. You don't have to do anything to earn it—all you have to do is receive it. That's the way God offers forgiveness. He extends it to you as a gift. You cannot earn your salvation.

Note the *wages* of sin is death. Death is something you can earn through repeated disobedience and rejection of God's forgiveness. You can earn the consequences for disobedience, but you can never earn forgiveness. It is God's free gift—His living water. The only thing you have to do to receive forgiveness is to receive forgiveness. And when you do, you truly have made a choice for life.

I invite you to read carefully the words of an Old Testament prophet who knew about the nature of sin, guilt, and the obstinacy of the human will when it is turned against God. This prophet, Daniel, wrote profoundly about sin, yet with the hope and belief that God does and will forgive. Let his words speak to your heart today. Make them your prayer:

> Then I set my face toward the Lord God to make request by prayer and supplications, with fasting, sackcloth, and ashes. And I prayed to the LORD my God, and made confession, and said, "O LORD, great and awesome God, who keeps His covenant and mercy with those who love Him, and with those who keep His commandments, we have sinned and committed iniquity, we have done wickedly and rebelled, even by departing from Your precepts and Your judgments. Neither have we heeded Your servants the prophets, who spoke in Your name to our kings and our princes, to our fathers and all the people of the land. O Lord, righteousness belongs to You, but to us shame of face" (Daniel 9:3–7).

9. What does Daniel mean when he says he "set his face" toward God? How does this compare with the "shame of face" to which Daniel also refers?

10. What is Daniel's unspoken assumption concerning God's mercy in this prayer? How does this apply to your need for forgiveness?

TODAY AND TOMORROW

Today: God's forgiveness is a gift, and there is nothing that I can ever do to earn it.

Tomorrow: I will praise the Lord for His free gift of my salvation.

CLOSING PRAYER

Heavenly Father, let us never try to downplay or discount the impact of our sin. We know that our sin separates us from You—and we desire to be in continual fellowship with You. Thank You for providing so much at Your expense—and nothing at our expense—so that we can be free from the penalty of the evil we have done. We humble ourselves before You, thank You for Your forgiveness, and pray that the Holy Spirit would continue to lead us to confess our sins to You. We accept the promise of forgiveness that is in Your Word—for You said that whosoever calls on the name of the Lord shall be saved. We want to receive Your life. Amen.

Notes and Prayer Requests

Use this space to write any key points, questions, or prayer requests from this week's study.

LESSON 5

What About the Christian Who Sins?

IN THIS LESSON

Learning: Does it mean that I'm not saved if I commit sin?

Growing: Will God ever forgive me for what I've done since being saved?

A saved person can commit sin—and he or she can also be forgiven. Christians who engage in sin tend to think one of two things. On the one hand, there are those Christians who say, "Well, I'm saved, so I have eternal security and am going to heaven. God will automatically forgive me of any sins I commit." On the other hand, there are those Christians who say, "I can't believe I did that as a Christian. How can God forgive me for this? I don't deserve a second chance (or a third chance or a hundredth chance). I'm going to sin again, so how can God ever forgive me?" In this lesson, we will take a look at both of these approaches.

A License to Sin?

Once we have received the Holy Spirit, He does not depart from us. God never stops loving us and never relinquishes His hold when we turn to Him and receive His forgiveness and the indwelling of the Holy Spirit. The Lord may appear silent in our lives for a period of time. We may not feel God's presence in a strong way. Nevertheless, the Lord is present in our lives.

Consider the example of the children of Israel. They erred, made mistakes, sinned, repented, and sinned again. God chastised them, disciplined them, and gave their enemies victory over them on occasion to cause them to turn again to Him. Even so, they were always the children of God. They never stopped being His people.

The same is true for us as Christians today. We are fully adopted into the family of God, and God does not disinherit His children. We are not immune to chastisement, discipline, or correction. On the contrary, the Spirit will correct us whenever it is necessary to help us stay in line with God's best for us But we are not subject to abandonment. As Paul wrote:

> Who shall separate us from the love of Christ? Shall tribulation, or distress, or persecution, or famine, or nakedness, or peril, or sword? . . . For I am persuaded that neither death nor life, nor angels nor principalities nor powers, nor things present nor things to come, nor height nor depth, nor any other created thing, shall be able to separate us from the love of God which is in Christ Jesus our Lord (Romans 8:35, 38–39).

However, knowing we can never be separated from Christ's love does not give us a license to sin. Rather, it is an impetus to live a righteous life. If we are looking for a way to justify our sin, perhaps we should question whether we have ever really received Christ into our lives in the first place. God calls us to holy, righteous, obedient living. Once we understand forgiveness and the deadly penalty of being in an unpardoned state of sin, we won't want to breach our relationship with God. Our sins will be grievous to us . . . not enjoyable.

People sometimes misuse this verse: "If we confess our sins, He is faithful and just to forgive us our sins and to cleanse us from all unrighteousness" (1 John 1:9). They assume, "Well, I can sin and run to God and ask Him to forgive me, and He will." That is a very casual attitude to have about a matter as serious as sin.

Yes, God will forgive us of our sins when we confess them, but we should reconsider what confession really means. Confession means we admit to God we have erred, are genuinely sorry for what we have done, and have no desire to commit the sin in the future. The confession should include a request that God, by the power of His Holy Spirit, will help us never to commit such a sin again.

1. "If You, Lord, should mark iniquities, O Lord, who could stand? But there is forgiveness with You, that You may be feared" (Psalm 130:3–4). The "fear" the psalmist mentions is a reverential awe toward God. Why is this a natural response to God's forgiveness?

2. "He who covers his sins will not prosper, but whoever confesses and forsakes them will have mercy" (Proverbs 28:13). How would you define *confession*? What does this verse say you need to do when you commit a sin?

Forgiveness Produces a Conduct Change

Prior to receiving Jesus Christ as our Savior, we had a natural tendency to sin. Sin was automatic for us. However, once we received the life of Christ, it was no longer natural for us to sin. Our nature now is to walk in close relationship with God. That is part of what it means to be a "new creation" in Christ Jesus (2 Corinthians 5:17).

This doesn't mean we won't occasionally yield to temptation and commit sin against God or our fellow human beings, but the Holy Spirit will quickly convict us about that sin. Our sin will seem unnatural, odious, and undesirable to us. We will want to receive God's forgiveness and be reconciled to our heavenly Father.

3. "Therefore, if anyone is in Christ, he is a new creation; old things have passed away; behold, all things have become new. Now all things are of God, who has reconciled us to Himself through Jesus Christ, and has given us the ministry of reconciliation"

(2 Corinthians 5:17–18). What "old things" passed away when you became a Christian?

4. In practical terms, what does it mean to be a "new creation"? What does this suggest regarding temptation and sin?

Our Father Is a Forgiving Father

How do we know God will forgive us if we turn to Him in humility to confess and repent of our sin? For the answer, we can look to the most famous parable of Jesus. In my opinion, the parable of the prodigal son should be called the parable of the forgiving father. The message of the story is of love and forgiveness from start to finish, but we need to recognize the image of God as a loving Father is not one introduced by Jesus. It is a message throughout the Old Testament.

Moses knew the gracious love of God when the Lord told him His "Presence" would go with him and He would give him rest, even after the children of Israel made a golden calf as an idol to worship (see Exodus 33:14–23). Nehemiah prayed to God with the full expectation that God would hear his confession on behalf of the children of Israel, forgive their sin, and restore His people to Jerusalem (see Nehemiah 1:11). The psalmist spoke repeatedly of a forgiving God (see Psalms 51; 130). Daniel saw forgiveness and mercy as God's very nature (see Daniel 9:9). God's love never changes. His love and His desire to forgive are inseparable.

The parable of the forgiving father is found in Luke 15:11–24. Jesus tells two other teachings about forgiveness earlier in that same chapter. The first is the story of a man who has 100 sheep and loses one of them. He searches for the one lost sheep until he finds it. When he returns home with the lost sheep draped over his shoulders, he calls his friends and neighbors together and says, "Rejoice with me, for I have found my sheep which was lost!" (verse 6).

The second story is about a woman who has ten silver coins. She loses one of them and searches diligently until she finds it. When she has recovered her precious coin, she calls her friends and neighbors together and says, "Rejoice with me, for I have found the piece which I lost!" In both cases, Jesus concludes His parables by saying, "There is joy in heaven over sinners who repent" (verses 9–10).

Jesus then tells a third story about a man with two sons. The younger son goes to his father and asks for his inheritance. They father agrees, and the son sets out for a far country, where he spends the money in wild living. When the money runs out, the son is forced to get a job feeding pigs—and is so hungry he longs to eat the pigs' food. Finally, the son comes to his senses and decides to return home, hoping his father will take him back as a servant.

But while the younger son is still a great way off, his father sees him and runs toward him. He hugs his wayward son and kisses him. The son says, "Father, I have sinned against heaven and in your sight, and am no longer worthy to be called your son" (verse 21). But the father says to his servants, "Bring out the best robe and put it on him, and put a ring on his hand and sandals on his feet. And bring the fatted calf here and kill it, and let us eat and be merry; for this my son was dead and is alive again; he was lost and is found" (verse 24).

Notice the son is part of the family. He is a good Jewish boy in a good Jewish family. As Christians, our identity can be with this son. He sinned even though he was part of the family. Likewise, we sometimes sin even though we are part of God's family.

5. What role does the father play in the son's forgiveness? What role does the son play?

6. Why does the father respond with such joy and generosity when his son returns? How would you have responded if you were the father? If you were the son?

THE MOTIVATION FOR GOD'S FORGIVENESS

The motivation for forgiveness lies squarely with the father. The younger son says, "I want what I want, and I want it now." He then leaves home with the inheritance his father gives him. And let me point out the father gave the boy what was going to be legally and rightfully his one day. He didn't deny the boy's request. He didn't override the boy's will. He let the boy go.

Just the father in this story, God will let you go today if you decide to turn your back on Him and walk away. He will continue to pursue you in the deep recesses of your heart and mind. But the Lord will never overstep the boundaries of your will to choose what and whom you want to pursue.

The boy walks away from the goodness and security he has known in his father's house—and in so doing, walks out of the will of God. He squanders what he has in loose living, which implies immoral indulgences. He squanders his inheritance—money his father earned. In other words, he has totally wasted all he once possessed of the father. In our terms today, we would probably conclude this boy was as backslidden as a person can get. He has no semblance of Christlikeness left in his behavior. He has lost it all. In his sin, he has wasted anything he had ever possessed in the way of an inheritance from the father.

Notice that after the boy squanders his inheritance, he faces a severe famine. Let me assure you, any time you walk out of the will of God, you *will* walk into a famine—a time of great need. The boy ends up feeding hogs, the most despicable job any good Jewish boy could have, since hogs are considered unclean by the Jews. Not only that, but in those days the Romans who occupied the land sacrificed hogs to the god of the netherworld. Their sacrifice was intended to pacify the devil himself. Do you get a picture of just how far this boy has gone from his father and from God?

There is nothing in what this boy has done to earn or motivate God's forgiveness. But the same is true for all of us. There is no task or good work we can do to earn our salvation. Nothing in us is commendable to God. The motivation for forgiving this errant son lies totally within the father, just as the motivation for forgiving sinners lies totally within God.

If you, as a born-again child of God, have sinned and turned from God, there is no good deed you can do to win yourself back into God's good graces. You can't substitute church attendance, witnessing, committee work, or any form of service for confession of your sins, a request for God's forgiveness, and repentance (a change of your mind and behavior).

7. When have you acted like the son in this parable? What was the result of your actions?

8. Put the son's prayer of repentance into your own words. Have you prayed something similar in your own life?

THE MANIFESTATION OF GOD'S FORGIVENESS

Notice in this story all the ways that the father responds to what his son has done. *First, the father sees the son while he is still a long way off.* The implication is the father is looking for him. The father certainly hasn't forgotten his son.

Second, the father has compassion. His heart is filled with love and concern. There is no hint this father has turned against his son or feels anything other than great affection toward him.

Third, the father runs to him. It was considered beneath the stature of a wealthy landowner to run—but this father runs to his son. He is eager to embrace his son and welcome him home. He has been waiting in forgiveness for his boy to return home.

Fourth, the father falls on his son's neck and kisses him. The father embraces his son fully and kisses him repeatedly, in Middle Eastern fashion. He is ecstatic at his son's return, and his heart overflows with love. There is no judgment toward his younger son. There are no demands for restitution or accounting. On the contrary, there is no hint of anything but warm acceptance.

Fifth, the father orders the servants to bring out the best robe for his son, a ring for the son's hand, and sandals for his feet. All of these signal the boy is a son and not a servant. This boy has just returned from a long journey and has come from a debauched lifestyle in which he was slopping hogs. He no doubt smells and looks like the reprobate person he has been. But the father covers all that with a fine robe. He is not going to have others gawking at his son and belittling him. He immediately restores him to a position of respect. He doesn't say, "Get yourself cleaned up and then we'll talk." He says, "Put a robe on my son. The past is the past."

The ring is no doubt a signet ring, which the boy could use to conduct business on his father's behalf. It is as if the father has given his son his personal charge card. The sandals send a signal the father has no intention of regarding his son in any way other than as a son. In that time, sandals were reserved for family members. All of these gifts are signs the father sees his son as a son, a fully restored member of his family. There is nothing that this boy has to do to earn or win his way back into the good graces of his father.

Sixth, the father tells his servants to kill the fatted calf and prepare a party. The father celebrates the fact his son has returned home. In an echo of the shepherd who lost a sheep and the woman who lost a valuable coin, this father says, "Let us eat and be merry; for this my son was dead and is alive again; he was lost and is found" (Luke 15:23–24). The father fully expects his son to remain with him and be a faithful son in every regard.

The father is unceasing in his love, patient in his waiting, and willing in his forgiveness. He is loving in his acceptance and ecstatic at his son's return. He restores his son completely, holding nothing back—faultlessly, asking for no accounting. Is this your image of your heavenly Father when you sin against Him? Do you see the Father as eager, longing, and completely willing for your return? All too often we see God as our judge who is waiting to punish us. Jesus said God is a loving Father, just waiting to forgive us for the wrongs that we have done.

I want you to recognize in this story that the father never holds any unforgiveness in his heart. He forgives his son when he asks for his inheritance, when he walks out the door, all the time that he is away, upon his return, and in his restoration. The father forgives his son the moment the son begins to move away. The father is forgiving at all times.

So is our heavenly Father. He never stops forgiving us. We are the ones who turn from the commandments that He has given to us. We are the ones who reject His forgiveness. We are the ones who walk away from His presence. So the question is not, "Will God forgive me, a Christian, when I sin?" The question is, "Will I receive God's forgiveness for my sin?"

9. "You have put off the old man with his deeds, and have put on the new man who is renewed in knowledge according to the image of Him who created him" (Colossians 3:9–10). What does it mean to "put off the old man"? Who is the "new man"?

10. In practical terms, how do we put off the old man? How do we put on the new man?

TODAY AND TOMORROW

Today: God is always forgiving, always working to bring us back to Himself.

Tomorrow: I will run back to my Father when I sin, knowing that He will receive me.

CLOSING PRAYER

Heavenly Father, thank You for the promise that nothing will ever separate Your children from the love You have for them. Thank You for the example in Scripture of the children of Israel, who erred, made mistakes, sinned against You, and repented—and You restored them. Like them, we know that we will never cease being Your children. Help us today to return to You when we sin like the prodigal returned to his father, knowing that You are ready, willing, and eager to forgive us and restore us. Thank You for always bringing us back to Yourself. Amen.

Notes and Prayer Requests

Use this space to write any key points, questions, or prayer requests from this week's study.

LESSON 6

What Role Does Confession Play?

IN THIS LESSON

Learning: What is the difference between repentance and confession?

Growing: Will God keep forgiving me again and again?

You may be saying at this point, "Well, what is our part? Isn't there anything we have to do?" Yes, we must do something as part of the process of receiving forgiveness.

The pattern for receiving forgiveness is evident in the story of the forgiving father. Remember, in the story the boy "came to himself" (Luke 15:17). We might say, "He came to his senses." He began to think the right way, and he began to have a clear picture of himself, his sin, and his father. He started to think the truth about his situation—that even his father's servants were better off than he was. Furthermore, his attitude was summed up in this statement: "Father, I have sinned against heaven and in your sight" (verse 18).

Recognizing the truth—and agreeing with it—is called *confession*. Confession is vital to receiving forgiveness. To *confess* means to "agree." It involves your thinking and admitting to God, "You're right, I've sinned. I'm a sinner. I have not only wronged other people and myself, but I have wronged heaven."

As long as you refuse to admit that you have done wrong, you can't be forgiven. God is certainly willing to forgive you. But if you refuse to admit that you have done wrong, you won't turn to Him and receive His forgiveness.

THE PURPOSE OF CONFESSION

I have cited this verse before, but it's worth repeating: "If we confess our sins, He is faithful and just to forgive us our sins and to cleanse us from all unrighteousness" (1 John 1:9). The process of being restored to a right fellowship with God begins when you confess your sins. It begins when you admit to God that you have done wrong and you recognize that you are out of fellowship with Him.

Of course, God already knows you have done wrong. He knew what you did the moment you did it. He knows your thoughts, motivations, intent, and will. Furthermore, if you are a Christian and you sin, God has already forgiven you. In Romans 8:1, Paul writes, "There is therefore now no condemnation to those who are in Christ Jesus, who do not walk according to the flesh, but according to the Spirit." Your confession doesn't cause God to forgive you. In confessing, you aren't talking God into forgiveness.

Any time Paul referred to *forgiveness* in his letters, he put it in the past tense. He reminded the Ephesians that Christ "forgave" them and they were "sealed" by the Holy Spirit (see 4:30–32). He reminded the Colossians they were the elect of God and "raised" with Christ (see 3:1). God has already forgiven you. No amount of confessing can talk God into something that is already His desire.

So, what is the purpose of confession if God already knows you have sinned and is willing to forgive you? The purpose is for you to come to grips with what you have done and the position you are in. Confession is a reality check. It's the key to your receiving forgiveness and experiencing the freedom that forgiveness brings.

If you do not admit to yourself and to God what you have done, you will not experience what God desires to give you: release from guilt and shame and new freedom to walk boldly in your relationship with Him. You confess so you can experience the forgiveness that has been available to you all along, enter fully into fellowship with God, and correct your behavior.

Let's say that I left my watch on the pulpit, and you come along and take it as your own. You know you've stolen the watch, and you feel a little uneasy about it, but you aren't too concerned because you don't think your sin will ever be revealed. Word comes to me that you have my watch, and my response is one of immediate forgiveness. I refuse to hold this act against you. I choose to cancel any debt associated with your deed.

Remember, that is what forgiveness is—a release and cancellation of any debt. Because I have forgiven you and freed you of any debt, I assume the loss of my watch. The person who forgives always assumes this loss. It's part of canceling the debt. Because I have canceled any debt regarding your wrongdoing, I can meet you in the hallway of the church and be friendly and warm with you. As far as I am concerned, your action is without any consequence to me.

Then someone comes to you and says, "The pastor knows you stole his watch." You are likely to be uncomfortable—even more so than you were before. You knew you were the thief, but you didn't know anybody else knew—and you certainly didn't know that I knew about it. Suddenly, you do whatever you can to avoid me. You feel strange in my presence.

Your friend comes to you again and says, "The pastor has forgiven you for stealing his watch." That has little impact on you. You think, "Well, maybe he has, but I'm not certain." Your sin continues to fester until you can't stand it any longer. Finally, you come to me and say, "Pastor, here's your watch. I took it from the pulpit, and I'm sorry. I know I've done wrong."

We have a time of reconciliation. I have already forgiven you, but now you are able to receive my forgiveness. Our fellowship is restored. In all likelihood, we are closer than ever.

1. "Confess your trespasses to one another, and pray for one another, that you may be healed. The effective, fervent prayer of a righteous man avails much" (James 5:16). When have you confessed a sin to another person? How did it affect your relationship?

2. When has someone confessed a sin to you? Did you forgive that person? How did it affect your relationship?

Asking for God's Forgiveness

Asking for God's forgiveness is likely to be part of your confession. In Jesus' parable, the prodigal son did not ask directly for his father to forgive him. But the request was implied in his saying, "Make me like one of your hired servants." The son didn't expect his father would restore him completely, but he did believe his father would take him back as a hired servant. In so doing, his father would have forgiven him to a degree. The heavenly Father knows that in your confession you are implicitly asking for Him to forgive you. Even so, you benefit by asking.

Jesus asked a blind man named Bartimaeus, "What do you want Me to do for you?" (Mark 10:51). Jesus could see Bartimaeus was blind. Bartimaeus knew that Jesus knew. Yet Jesus asked him the question anyway. The question was not for Jesus' information. It was for Bartimaeus' sake, that he would realize fully what he was requesting of God. With sight would come all sorts of responsibilities for Bartimaeus. He would have to work for his living rather than beg. He would have to be responsible for his care rather than rely on the constant help of others. Jesus no doubt wanted to make certain that Bartimaeus knew fully what he was asking.

The same holds true for us. When we state openly and directly what we have done as a sin, and we ask openly and directly for forgiveness of that sin, we are much more likely to face our sin and determine within ourselves that we will not sin again. In like manner, when we first come to the Lord for forgiveness, and we state openly that we are sinners, we are much more likely to determine that we will live our lives in a new way and walk in a new direction.

Asking for God's forgiveness does not force God to forgive you. He already has done so out of His unconditional love. But it does make you more acutely aware of what you are asking, who you are addressing when you make your request, and what might be the actions that God wants you to take.

3. "If you confess with your mouth the Lord Jesus and believe in your heart that God has raised Him from the dead, you will be saved. For with the heart one believes unto righteousness, and with the mouth confession is made unto salvation" (Romans

10:9–10). What role is played by the heart in confession? What role is played by the mouth? Why are both important?

....

....

....

....

....

....

4. What conditions must you fulfill to receive righteousness? To receive salvation?

....

....

....

....

....

....

....

The Importance of Asking with Faith

As you make your confession and ask God to forgive you, do so with faith, fully trusting God to hear your confession and to forgive you. *Believing* for forgiveness is a part of *receiving* forgiveness. If you don't believe God is going to forgive you, you won't receive forgiveness, and you won't experience freedom from guilt's bondage. You must believe that God is going to be true to His Word and forgive you when you confess your sins and ask Him for forgiveness.

If you have never confessed your sins to God, you must believe that when you do, God is going to hear your confession and immediately transfer you from the kingdom of darkness to the kingdom of God (see Acts 26:18). You must believe you are no longer a victim of Satan but a child of God. You must believe God has freed you from the bondage of sin and guilt and that you are now free to walk in full fellowship with Him.

If you are a Christian, when you confess your sin and ask God to forgive you, you must believe God has forgiven you and restored you to full fellowship with Him. It is by faith you can say to the Lord as you confess and ask for forgiveness, "I receive what Jesus Christ did for me on the cross. I receive Your forgiveness into my life. I receive the gift of Your Holy Spirit. I receive Your full embrace of love and Your call to follow You in the paths of righteousness."

5. "Ask, and it will be given to you; seek, and you will find; knock, and it will be opened to you. For everyone who asks receives, and he who seeks finds, and to him who knocks it will be opened" (Matthew 7:7–8). Why does Jesus speak of asking, seeking, and knocking regarding confession? What do these actions imply about confession of sin?

6. According to these verses, who will receive forgiveness? What guarantee do you have?

The Role of Repentance

To *repent* means to "change your mind and behavior." Repentance is an act of the will. It involves follow-through behavior. Confession is an admission; it is saying, "I have sinned." Repentance takes that confession and puts it into action. It is declaring, "I am changing my mind and my behavior so that I will not sin again." Repentance involves the actual doing of what you say you are going to do.

The prodigal son said, "I will arise and go to my father." Two verses later, we read, "He arose and came to his father" (verses 18, 20). The prodigal made a decision about a change in his behavior, which included a change in his circumstances and location, and then acted on that decision. That is repentance. Repentance doesn't bring you into a forgiven, guilt-free relationship with the Father. Confession and asking God to forgive you does that . . . but repentance keeps you there.

Too many people believe they must repent of their sins before God will forgive them. No! We repent of our sins *because* the Father forgives us. Our change of behavior doesn't happen before we come to God and receive His forgiveness. If that were the case, repentance would be filled with all sorts of works—good deeds to do, points to earn, obstacles to overcome. Our declaration that we intend to change our behavior and not sin again may be part of our confession, but the real change in our behavior comes *after* we have received God's forgiveness.

Thank God that it does, because when we are in full reconciliation with God, we are more likely to avail ourselves of the full power of the Holy Spirit working in us to help us stay true to our commitment. Repentance allows us to walk in abundant grace and in God's gift of righteousness, which He promises to us as part of our forgiveness (see Romans 5:17). Repentance is our decision to follow God, followed by our change of behavior that keeps us on God's path.

Honest confession admits sin and asks for God's forgiveness. Repentance defines a necessary change in behavior to live a righteous life—you make a declaration that you are going to pursue that change and then follow through with actual change. To confess without repentance is to say, "I'm sorry," without any effort to sin no more. Genuine repentance—the desire and action *not* to sin again—validates confession. The two are inseparable for any person who desires to walk in close fellowship with God.

7. When have you confessed a sin to the Lord without really intending to abandon that sin in the future? What was the result?

8. When have you determined in your heart to stop committing some sinful act in the future? What was the result?

Confession and Intimacy with God

Confession should be continual. Any time you recognize sin in your life, you must come to God and confess it. This isn't so your salvation can be kept current and up-to-date, but so you can live and walk in continual freedom and intimacy with the Father. Each time you sin, you should confess it to God and ask His forgiveness. But if you are involved in repeated confessions for the same type of behavior, you should ask, "Have I really repented of this? Am I making the effort to change my mind and my behavior? Am I relying on the Holy Spirit to help me *not* to sin?"

To sin repeatedly is an act of your will. So is repentance. Your will is within your power. You *can* change your mind, your behavior, your actions, and your words, and if you ask the Holy Spirit to help you, He will! On the other hand, you need to confess a specific act of sin only once. God will hear your confession and forgive you. It doesn't matter how awful or how big your sin has been—God is able to forgive it in one moment!

Ultimately, full confession has to do with restoring and maintaining intimacy with God. The Lord wants to walk in close fellowship with you today. He longs to have a walking-and-talking-together relationship with you.

So confess to the Lord you have done things, said things, thought things, and believed things that make you uncomfortable in His presence. Ask Him to forgive you for your sins and to remove your feelings of guilt and discomfort in His presence. Believe in faith that He not only hears your request but also grants it fully. And then walk with the Lord! Talk to Him. Share your life with Him, and invite Him to share His life with you.

9. "The Lord is not slack concerning His promise, as some count slackness, but is longsuffering toward us, not willing that any should perish but that all should come to repentance" (2 Peter 3:9). When has the Lord been longsuffering toward you?

10. To what "promise" is Peter referring? How have you claimed that promise in your life?

TODAY AND TOMORROW

Today: God is always forgiving, even when I am still in sin.

Tomorrow: I will be more faithful in repenting of sin, not just in confessing it.

Closing Prayer

Thank You, Lord, for loving us so graciously, kindly, and undeservedly. Thank You that You are the one who pursues us and extends the offer of forgiveness to us. Today, we ask that You would help us to confess our sins to You, knowing that it is for our benefit. Release us from the guilt and shame of our sins so we can find freedom and walk boldly in our relationship with You. Correct us and discipline us in those areas of our lives where we are not following You in the way we should. Continually lead us to confession so that our fellowship may be restored and we may walk in greater intimacy with You. Amen.

Notes and Prayer Requests

Use this space to write any key points, questions, or prayer requests from this week's study.

LESSON 7

Forgiving Undeserved Injuries

IN THIS LESSON

Learning: Why should I forgive a person who hurts me unjustly?

Growing: How can I let go of past hurts?

Unforgiveness is an issue that nearly all of us have to deal with at some point. Unforgiveness that is allowed to remain in our spirits is both painful and destructive. I consider it to be the major root of many physical, emotional, and spiritual problems today.

The apostle Paul wrote to the Ephesians, "Let all bitterness, wrath, anger, clamor, and evil speaking be put away from you, with all malice. And be kind to one another, tenderhearted, forgiving one another, even as God in Christ forgave you" (4:31–32). Paul was describing the manifestations of a "spirit of unforgiveness" when he spoke of bitterness, wrath, anger, clamor, and evil speaking. A spirit of unforgiveness goes beyond a temporary state of unforgiveness, which is the period between the time a person is hurt and the time he or she forgives the one who caused the hurt. A spirit of unforgiveness develops when the person chooses to remain in a state of unforgiveness toward the other person.

A spirit of unforgiveness is summed up in this remark: "I don't think I could ever forgive that person." We feel we have been dealt with in such an unjust way that we can't let go of the pain. But we need to face the fact we are all going to be hurt. We have been hurt, are hurting now, or are going to be hurt by somebody in some area. The only way we can insulate ourselves against being hurt is to remove ourselves completely from the possibility of love. To risk love is to risk hurt.

Unforgiveness is a choice that we make with the will—and it's a bad choice.

Unforgiveness Is Hatred

Unforgiveness is actually a form of hatred. You may say, "I don't hate anybody." By this, you probably mean you wouldn't murder anybody or do anything intentionally to harm another person. But ask yourself: "Do I avoid encountering a certain person? Do I find it difficult to speak well of a certain person? Does the very thought of a particular person make me cringe or clench my fist?" If your answer is yes, you are harboring hatred in the form of unforgiveness.

Hatred exists in degrees. An unforgiving spirit is marked by hatred. You will know that you have such a spirit if you can't shake the painful memory of a hurt done to you, You can't honestly wish the offending person well, or you want the other person to feel pain and suffering to the degree that you have felt them. If this describes you, face up to the fact you have a degree of hatred in you for that person—and you have a spirit of unforgiveness.

Eventually, that spirit of unforgiveness will take one of two forms in your life. You will either stuff it inside you and keep it bottled up, where it will turn to bitterness and resentment, or you will actively seek to retaliate against the person, taking vengeance in your own hands to repay the wrong done to you. Either way, you will be the victim of your unforgiveness far more than the person who has wronged you. However, there is a way out! Nobody can make you have an unforgiving spirit. It is an act of your will. You can choose by your will to forgive.

You *should* choose to forgive for your own health and well-being, but it is also important to note that God *commands* you to make that choice. God's commandments are always for your good, and this one is no exception. Jesus plainly taught, "If you forgive men their trespasses, your heavenly Father will also forgive you. But if you do not forgive men their trespasses, neither will your Father forgive your trespasses" (Matthew 6:14–15). If you want to experience God's forgiveness, you must forgive others.

1. Has a particular person or past injury come to your mind? Is the Lord showing you an area of unforgiveness? How will you act on that prompting?

2. "Love your enemies, do good to those who hate you, bless those who curse you, and pray for those who spitefully use you. To him who strikes you on the one cheek, offer the other also" (Luke 6:27–29). What sorts of injuries are covered by these verses? Which of them have been done to you? Which have you done to others?

....

....

....

....

....

....

Reasons for an Unforgiving Spirit

There are three main reasons people have an unforgiving spirit. The first reason is *pride*. We don't want to forgive because we believe that in some way, forgiving the other person will diminish us. We're afraid people will think we're weak. In other cases, we may not want to admit we've been hurt or confess we are finding it difficult to forgive. We fear people will look down on us for feeling hurt or having an area of weakness in our spiritual lives. And in still other cases, we may enjoy the attention we receive from others who know we have been wronged. To forgive would be to step out of the limelight of their concern.

A second reason is *control*. This is closely linked to pride. We want to make sure the person who has wronged us is punished in the way we choose. The only way that we can ensure that is to hold on to the person, even if it's only holding on to the person in our hearts. We refuse to let go and leave the person in God's hands.

A third reason is *ignorance*. Some people don't know how to respond to old hurts and painful situations. They have never been taught how to forgive—so they haven't forgiven. Others have a faulty understanding of what it means to forgive. Also, nonbelievers find it difficult to forgive others fully because they have not experienced forgiveness from God. God's forgiveness is the model for our forgiveness of others. And in part, it is because of the power of the Holy Spirit in our lives that we are enabled to forgive and release another person fully.

If you are struggling today with unforgiveness, ask yourself why you refuse to free the other person. What compels you to hang on to that hurt and memory?

3. "What comes out of a man, that defiles a man. For from within, out of the heart of men, proceed evil thoughts, adulteries, fornications, murders, thefts, covetousness, wickedness, deceit, lewdness, an evil eye, blasphemy, pride, foolishness. All these evil things come from within and defile a man" (Mark 7:20–23). In what way do these sins come "from within"?

4. How does this principle apply to bitterness versus forgiveness? What is within us that produces bitterness? What is within us that produces forgiveness?

Our Hurt Can Cause Us to Hurt Others

Our pride and desire for control are at the heart of our trying to have the upper hand over the person who has wronged us. Our hurt can also cause us to take out our bitterness and resentment on others—even those who may not have hurt us directly. Jesus taught the following parable to illustrate this point:

> Therefore the kingdom of heaven is like a certain king who wanted to settle accounts with his servants. And when he had begun to settle accounts, one was brought to him who owed him ten thousand talents. But as he was not able to pay, his master commanded that he be sold, with his wife and children and all that he had, and that payment be made. The servant therefore fell down before him, saying, "Master, have patience with me, and I will pay you all." Then the master of that servant was moved with compassion, released him, and forgave him the debt.
>
> But that servant went out and found one of his fellow servants who owed him a hundred denarii; and he laid hands on him and took him by the throat, saying, "Pay me what you owe!" So his fellow servant fell down at his feet and begged him, saying, "Have patience with me, and I will pay you all." And he would not, but went and threw him into prison till he should pay the debt. So when his fellow servants saw what had been done, they were very grieved, and came and told their master all that had been done. Then the master, after he had called him, said to him, "You wicked servant! I forgave you all that debt because you begged me. Should you not also have had compassion on your fellow servant, just as I had pity on you?" And his master was angry, and delivered him to the torturers until he should pay all that was due to him.
>
> So My heavenly Father also will do to you if each of you, from his heart, does not forgive his brother his trespasses (Matthew 18:23–35).

No one has a right to harbor unforgiveness and cause harm to another person. The cross strips us of that right. Jesus Christ was pure, sinless, and without any shadow of deceit, yet He died on the cross to forgive us. We have no right to deny that forgiveness to another person who is in the same position we have been in: a sinner in need of forgiveness and salvation.

Forgiveness of others is essential. There may be excuses for us to harbor unforgiveness, but no excuse is a justifiable reason before our heavenly Father. He *commands* us to forgive.

5. Which servant in this parable do you sympathize with more: the one forgiven by the king, or the who owed a hundred denarii? Which servant do you *resemble* more?

6. Why did the king forgive the servant who owed him ten thousand talents? Why did he throw him into prison later?

Dealing with Issues of Unforgiveness

As we close, I will first list four consequences of an unforgiving spirit and then explain how to deal with any issues of unforgiveness. *The first consequence is emotional bondage.* Your memories may torment you, causing you to relive the pain you have experienced. You likely will find that you have little capacity to love others or to receive love. Intimacy may be difficult for you.

The second consequence is damaged relationships with others. You will have relationships marked by anger and fighting—sometimes with what seem to be volcanic eruptions.

The third consequence is a damaged relationship with the Lord. The Holy Spirit will bring your unforgiveness to your mind until you deal with it. You will feel restlessness and uneasiness in your spirit until you do. The Holy Spirit cannot anoint unforgiveness, so your ability to minister to others will be stunted.

The fourth consequence is a damaged physical being. Unforgiveness puts an overload on the nervous system, and eventually a fuse will blow in some area of your body. God did not design the physical body to endure the long-standing stress caused by a spirit of unforgiveness.

The first step in dealing with a spirit of unforgiveness is to identify the person who has hurt you. I suggest you weigh carefully whether to confront a person about the hurt caused to you. Your parents, for example, have probably done the best they knew how in raising you, and confronting them with old hurts is only going to wound them. Your dealings with your hurt should never bring hurt to someone else.

So conduct a confrontation with the person "by proxy." Take two chairs—one for you, and an empty one to represent the other person. Sit down and talk to that empty chair as if the person is sitting in it. Be true to your feelings. Let out your hurt. You may cry, shout, even kick the chair! Don't hold anything back. In the course of speaking to the "person," identify the hurt you feel. Be specific in how you feel and how much you hurt. Identify the debt—cite examples, such as places, times, events, and conversations in which the person hurt you.

You may need several sessions to let out all your pain, and your conversation may last for several hours. Spend whatever time it takes to air your full grievance against the person. Then draw a line between all you have said of your pain and the hurt that has occurred in the past. Declare, "By the grace of God, I release you today. I refuse to hold these things in my heart and memory any longer. I choose to be free of the pain that you have caused me."

Ask the Lord to help you. Confess to Him that you have harbored a spirit of unforgiveness. Ask Him to forgive you. Ask Him to release you of the pain as you take these steps. And believe, by faith, that

He will do so. Choose to take a new direction in your life—one that is free of pain and bondage associated with old hurts.

7. "Pursue peace with all people, and holiness, without which no one will see the Lord: looking carefully lest anyone fall short of the grace of God; lest any root of bitterness springing up cause trouble, and by this many become defiled" (Hebrews 12:14–15). What is a "root of bitterness"? How is it rooted out?

8. How does a root of bitterness cause people to become defiled? Give practical examples.

The Results of Forgiveness

If you continue to think of things the hurtful party has said or done, do the exercise again. If other people come to mind, give them a turn in the empty chair. If you have a spirit of unforgiveness, you may need to forgive several people. Deal with each person who has hurt you. Here are some of the results of taking this act of your will:

First, your memory will begin to be healed. You will think less often of the offending person, and each time with less hurt.

Second, you will begin to see the person that you have forgiven in a new light. You are likely to see the person you have forgiven as a sinner in need of God's forgiveness, and you likely will have more compassion for him or her.

Third, you will begin to experience freedom in your emotions and in your ability to relate to other people. You are no longer in bondage to that person, and you are likely to feel free to relate to other people more readily. If you have been afraid to risk loving another person, you likely will have the courage and strength to take that risk.

Fourth, you may also experience reconciliation with the person that you have forgiven. That isn't always the case, but sometimes it is possible for there to be a coming together again in friendship or love.

Again, if you choose to remain in unforgiveness, the effects are like a slow poison that works in the soul. An unforgiving spirit is always corruptive, destructive, and degenerative. Choose to be free of the bondage associated with unforgiveness. Choose to forgive!

9. "Beloved, do not avenge yourselves, but rather give place to wrath; for it is written, 'Vengeance is mine, I will repay,' says the Lord. Therefore 'If your enemy is hungry, feed him; if he is thirsty, give him a drink; for in so doing you will heap coals of fire on his head'" (Romans 12:19–20). What does it mean to "give place to wrath"? How is this the opposite of vengeance?

10. What does it mean to "heap coals of fire" on your enemy's head? How is this different from seeking revenge?

TODAY AND TOMORROW

Today: It is vitally important that I root out bitterness and forgive others.

Tomorrow: I will ask the Lord to show me where a root of bitterness might be growing.

Closing Prayer

Father, it is so easy to fall into the trap of bitterness and be so filled with resentment. We feel wronged, hurt, abused, used, misused—and the hurt is so deep and the roots are growing every day. Today, we ask that You give us the courage to acknowledge our pain, to confess our unforgiveness, to repent of it, to lay it all out, to open our grip, and to recognize that if we are just willing to set the other person free, all the shackles will fall aside. We want to release the weight on our lives—to breathe better, sleep better, see better, hear better, speak better—and allow Your grace to flow with beauty into our hearts and through our lives. This is our prayer today: free us from the snare of an unforgiving spirit. We pray this in Jesus' name. Amen.

Notes and Prayer Requests

Use this space to write any key points, questions, or prayer requests from this week's study.

LESSON 8

Developing a Forgiving Spirit

IN THIS LESSON

Learning: Why do I keep coming around to struggling with resentment again?

Growing: How can I break the cycle of unforgiveness and forgiveness?

As I have stated several times in this study, forgiveness is an act of the will. It's difficult to operate in a rational way, out of the will, when we are being swallowed up by painful and sometimes agonizing emotions. When we are wronged, our natural instinct is to blast our way out of the hurt (with an outburst of anger and hatred) or to bury the hurt (resulting in eventual bitterness and resentment).

The good news is that we can trust the Holy Spirit to help us not act on our natural instincts. In those brief moments before we cry, explode, or steel ourselves against the oncoming pain, we can breathe a quick prayer and say, "Holy Spirit, help me to respond as Jesus would respond. Help me to forgive."

There seems to be a twelve-part cycle of unforgiveness and forgiveness that many people experience. In this lesson, I will describe each of the steps to you. I will begin with the initial stages in the cycle (steps 1-9) and then explore the later stages (steps 10–12). From there, we will examine the Sinner's Cycle, the Christian's Cycle of Self-Recrimination and Self-Forgiveness, and then look at ways for how to shorten each of the stages.

Early Stages in the Cycle of Unforgiveness

The first step in the cycle is that we feel wronged. We feel hurt by another person, who may have committed a trespass against us intentionally or unintentionally. The person does not even have to have sinned against us for us to feel hurt. The hurt is our response to a situation, event, or conversation. We may feel wronged whether we should feel that way or not.

Second, we have difficulty dealing with our hurt. The hurt lingers. The situation matters to us—the pain is great and the suffering is ongoing. We struggle with our feelings.

Third, we try to take a detour away from the hurt. Our first response when we are hurt is to flee. We want the pain to go away, so we try to move away from it. We try various substitutes to forgiveness in order to feel better.

Fourth, we deny the pain. We try to convince ourselves the hurt doesn't matter or that we aren't really hurting.

Fifth, we dig a hole for the pain. When we discover we cannot outmaneuver our pain—either by taking a detour away from it or denying it—we attempt to bury it. We refuse to talk about it and try to forget it. We repress the pain.

Sixth, we feel defeated. We conclude the person who offended us has scored a victory over us. We have a sense of bitterness and resentment about that. By this point, in all likelihood we have developed a spirit of unforgiveness.

Seventh, we experience defilement. The pain we have buried within us taints or stains (defiles) our relationships with others. We have shorter tempers and less compassion toward others. We are less willing to risk giving and receiving love.

Eighth, we become discouraged about life. Without freedom in our ability to relate to others, and without freedom and a sense of victory in ourselves, we become discouraged and may even become clinically depressed. We experience no peace on the inside or the outside.

Ninth, we become desperate. The pain continues to simmer inside us until we reach the point where we are desperate for relief. We want a way out of our misery. At this stage, we are in a very vulnerable state. We are likely to act irrationally and without clear discernment. This is a dangerous state and mindset in which to live.

1. When is a time when you had difficulty dealing with a hurt, tried to take a detour from it, and then denied or tried to bury the pain? What was the result?

2. When is a time you felt defeated by the hurt, experienced defilement in a relationship, and then became discouraged and desperate? How did you cope during that time?

Later Stages in the Cycle of Unforgiveness

At this point in the cyclewe come to a choice that we must make on how we will move forward. *For this tenth stage in the cycle, we can either enter into destructive behavior or attempt to discover the cause of our pain.*

People who are desperate often enter into destructive behaviors. They may turn to drugs, alcohol, pain killers, sleeping pills, or other avenues for would-be relief from pain—a course of action that leads only to the further pain of addiction. Those who are desperate sometimes seek to escape the life they have known. They may seek divorce, run away, join communes filled with other desperate people, or engage in occult practices. They may even commit suicide. Each avenue is a manifestation of self-destructive behavior.

Outright destructive behavior may also occur. People may take revenge on the person whom they regard as the source of their pain. They may cause the person physical harm or do everything within their power to destroy the person's reputation. Fortunately, not all who are desperate choose avenues of destruction. In their desperation, some choose to turn to therapy and counseling to get to the root cause of their pain. They turn to God, church, prayer groups, Bible studies, or to the Word of God for solace, advice, and relief of their pain.

People who choose the destructive course nearly always recognize they have chosen a dead-end avenue, and they eventually turn to counseling, therapy, or other positive means of discovery. Ultimately, the counsel of God's Word and the power of the Holy Spirit will free a person from this vicious cycle, so we must assume a person who is honestly seeking answers will be led by the Holy Spirit to godly counselors and godly wisdom. That certainly should be our prayer for ourselves or for others who find themselves in a desperate state and who begin to make a positive attempt to discover the root cause of their desperation.

This leads to the eleventh stage in the cycle: we begin to deal with the cause of our pain for what it is—a state of unforgiveness. Ultimately, the cause of our pain in this cycle is our inability or failure to forgive. We may struggle in our attempts to rationalize, justify, or explain the many reasons why we haven't forgiven another person. But in the end, each of us comes face-to-face with this fact that we have to forgive the other person to be free.

Finally, we experience deliverance from our pain as we forgive. We forgive and experience God's release from bondage, guilt, and the spirit of unforgiveness.

3. "'Be angry, and do not sin': do not let the sun go down on your wrath, nor give place to the devil" (Ephesians 4:26–27). What does it mean to not let the "sun go down on your wrath?" How does unforgiveness lead to destructive behaviors?

4. "And forgive us our debts, as we forgive our debtors" (Matthew 6:12). When is a time you realized you had to forgive another person in order to experience freedom?

The Sinner's Cycle of Unforgiveness

I have described this cycle in terms of forgiving another person, but the same cycle exists for sinners and for those who struggle to forgive themselves. Let me briefly give you those stages:

- *Wronged:* We have an awareness within our hearts that we are living in a state of sin with a nature of sin and are thus separated from God.
- *Struggle*: We struggle with the fact that we are sinners.
- *Detour*: We try to ignore the inner struggle.
- *Denial*: We try to convince ourselves we are not really sinners
- *Repression*: We try to avoid the issue and turn to other pursuits and activities.
- *Defeat*: We live with a sense that we never quite measure up. We may have wariness of others or an abiding sense of failure.
- *Defilement*: We are unable to enter fully into godly relationships. We avoid people that we perceive as "too spiritual" or ones who speak often of God.
- *Discouragement*: We have no peace inside. We feel inner tumult and a sense of futility about life.
- *Desperation*: We reach the point where we *must* do something about our feelings.
- *Destruction or discovery*. We turn and run from God as fast as we can, and as far as we can. Or we turn toward God and begin to explore who He is, what He has said, and why He loves us.
- *Dealing with the pain*. We face the fact that we are sinners in need of God's salvation. We confess this to ourselves and to God, ask Him for His forgiveness, and decide that we are going to live in accordance with His plan for our lives.
- *Deliverance*. We receive God's forgiveness and are delivered from sin and its guilt and pain. We begin a new life in fellowship with our heavenly Father and with the help of the Holy Spirit.

All sinners who come to the Father for forgiveness will go through this cycle, though not all will experience all stages as profoundly, and not all will linger as long in any one stage as others do.

5. Have you accepted God's free gift of forgiveness through Christ? If not, which step (from the previous page) are you on?

6. If you have received Christ as your Savior, what was the process by which you found deliverance from sin?

The Christian's Cycle of Self-Recrimination and Self-Forgiveness

Let's now look at the Christian's cycle of self-recrimination and self-forgiveness. Unlike the previous cycle we discussed, the focus of this cycle is on how believers in Christ come to recognize the fact of their sin, seek forgiveness, and then forgive themselves.

- *Wronged.* We have an awareness we have sinned against God.
- *Struggle.* We struggle with the fact that we have failed God after He has so generously forgiven us of our sinful nature and called us His children.
- *Detour.* We try to ignore the inner struggle that we feel and dismiss it.
- *Denial.* We try to convince ourselves we have not sinned significantly, or that God will forgive us automatically without any confession on our part.

- *Repression.* We continue in the Christian life as if nothing has happened.
- *Defeat.* We have a deep inner feeling that the enemy has defeated us or that we have defeated ourselves. We fear we may never have a fully restored relationship with God.
- *Defilement.* We are unable to minister to others freely.
- *Discouragement.* We become void of hope that things might ever get better.
- *Desperation.* We feel we *must* do something.
- *Destruction or discovery.* We run from God and God's people as fast as we can, or we turn toward God and begin to explore the possibility of His forgiveness.
- *Dealing with the pain.* We face the fact we have sinned before God. We believe that He will forgive us as we confess our sin to Him, ask for His forgiveness, make a decision to move forward in our lives, and, with help from the Holy Spirit, not sin again.
- *Deliverance.* We receive God's forgiveness, are delivered from our sin and the pain of our guilt and shame, and live in restored fellowship with the Father, according to His commandments.

7. When have you found it difficult to forgive yourself for something you have done? In what ways did you experience this cycle?

8. "I acknowledged my sin to You, and my iniquity I have not hidden. I said, 'I will confess my transgressions to the Lord,' and You forgave the iniquity of my sin" (Psalm 32:5). What is the assurance that you are given in this verse?

SHORTENING THE CYCLE

Many people take years to move through these stages. They may experience many sleepless nights and stress-related illnesses. Some spend a great deal of money in various pursuits to assuage their guilt or shame, while others spend thousands of dollars in therapy.

Is there a way to shorten this cycle? The answer is yes! You can move directly from stage 1 to stage 11—from feeling the pain of being wronged to dealing with the pain. You can refuse to take any detours or engage in denial. Instead, you can decide to confront your pain head-on and face it as an issue of forgiveness.

The way to do this is to first *pray to the Lord*, "Father, I have been hurt. Please heal my wounded heart. Heal me of these feelings of rejection, alienation, sorrow, and loss."

Next, *confess to the Lord*, "I confess that I want to retaliate against this person. I am angry, frustrated, and in pain. I know these emotions are not going to be helpful to me or resolve the situation. I ask You to forgive me of these negative feelings. I desire to forgive this person, Lord. Help me to forgive."

Finally, *declare before the Lord with faith*, "I free this person right now from the wrong that he or she has done against me. I let this person go and turn him or her over to You. You deal with the person, Lord. I turn over all responsibility to You. Free me from any memories that might haunt me or discourage me in the wake of this hurtful experience. Help me to walk in freedom and strength in relationship to this person and to all others who know of this incident. I trust You to do this, Holy Spirit. And I ask this in Jesus' name. Amen."

The more times you forgive others who hurt you, the more automatic your response will be to forgive. As you forgive and develop a forgiving spirit, you will find that compassion grows in your heart—compassion for those who are sinners, for those who have sinned against you, and for those who are struggling with a spirit of unforgiveness. You will find new opportunities to minister to people who are in the bondage of sin, guilt, shame, or unforgiveness.

If you do not forgive immediately and begin to move through the cycle of unforgiveness and forgiveness, you can stop at any stage and move directly to the stage of acknowledging your need to forgive. If you find yourself avoiding God, speaking words of denial, or feeling discouraged, you can go immediately to the Lord and admit your feelings, confess your unforgiveness, make a declaration of forgiveness for the other person, and receive God's healing, forgiveness, and freedom in your life.

You can turn to the Lord at any time . . . and the sooner the better!

9. "Therefore submit to God. Resist the devil and he will flee from you. Draw near to God and He will draw near to you" (James 4:7–8). In practical terms, how do you "resist the devil"? How is this done in the process of forgiveness?

....

....

....

....

....

....

10. "Cleanse your hands, you sinners; and purify your hearts, you doubleminded. Lament and mourn and weep! . . . Humble yourselves in the sight of the Lord, and He will lift you up" (James

4:9–10). What role does "cleansing" your hands, purfiying your heart, and humbling yourself before God play in forgiveness?

TODAY AND TOMORROW

Today: The cycle of forgiveness is shortened when I confront my pain and turn it over to God.

Tomorrow: I will take time this week to confront unresolved hurts and to forgive those who have hurt me.

CLOSING PRAYER

Heavenly Father, Your love for us is beyond comprehension. Thank You for keeping us. Thank You for guiding us. Thank You for providing grace that is absolutely beyond our ability to grasp. Thank You for showing us what really took place on the cross and what happens moment by moment in our lives as we walk in You and You walk in us. Take us today through the necessary steps so that we can develop a forgiving spirit. We desire that forgiving others be as natural to us and eating, sleeping, breathing, and walking. Thank You for the promise that You will never leave us nor forsake us. We praise You for Your presence in our lives. Amen.

Notes and Prayer Requests

Use this space to write any key points, questions, or prayer requests from this week's study.

LESSON 9

JOSEPH: A LIFE OF FORGIVENESS

IN THIS LESSON

Learning: Is it really possible to fully forgive people who have deeply injured me?

Growing: How can I make forgiveness part of my character, rather than bitterness?

God's Word gives us a great example of a person who embodied a forgiving spirit—a man named Joseph. If any person ever had just cause to be angry with his brothers and to allow a spirit of unforgiveness to develop, it was him. And yet we have no hint in the Scriptures that Joseph ever had such an unforgiving spirit.

Just consider some of the reasons that Joseph had to harbor unforgiveness in his heart. *First, he knew the hatred his brothers had toward him.* At the beginning of Joseph's story, when he is seventeen, we read how he shared with his brothers two prophetic dreams the Lord had given to him. In one dream, he and his brothers were in a grain field, binding sheaves, and the sheaves (representing his brothers) bowed down to his sheaf. In the second dream, the sun, moon, and eleven stars bowed down to Joseph. The Bible tells us his brothers "hated him and could not speak peaceably to him" (Genesis 37:4).

Second, Joseph was misunderstood by his father. When Joseph shared his dreams, his father, Jacob, rebuked him and said, "What is this dream that you have dreamed? Shall your mother and I and your brothers indeed come to bow down to the earth before you?" (verse 10). Joseph was the eleventh son and is described as the beloved son. I feel certain this rebuke from his father wounded him deeply.

Third, Joseph was badly mistreated by his brothers. When Joseph went to visit his brothers in Dothan, they saw him coming and plotted against him. They stripped him of his tunic, cast him into a pit, and then sat on the ground above, eating a meal—no doubt taunting Joseph. They intended to kill him, but when they saw a caravan of Midianites they decided to sell Joseph into slavery instead (see 37:12–28).

1. What are some of reasons Joseph had to harbor unforgiveness?

2. If you had been in Joseph's place, heading into slavery, how would you have felt? What would you have thought of your brothers?

Joseph in Potiphar's House

How do we know Joseph did not develop an unforgiving spirit in the aftermath of these events? Well, once he was in Egypt, a man named Potiphar, an officer of Pharaoh and captain of the guard, purchased Joseph and brought him into his home. We are told that Potiphar "saw that the Lord was with [Joseph] and that the Lord made all he did to prosper in his hand. So Joseph found favor in his sight, and served him. Then he made him overseer of his house, and all that he had he put under his authority" (Genesis 39:3–4).

Had Joseph been a man with an unforgiving spirit, he would have had a seething hatred inside him. Such a spirit eventually manifests itself in some way, usually in acts of rebellion. A person with an unforgiving spirit sometimes has a chip on the shoulder or a surly attitude. A slave with a rebellious attitude is not one you put in charge of your worldly goods or other slaves in your household. It is not a person to whom you entrust your wife and family. Potiphar, however, had complete confidence in Joseph.

Furthermore, Potiphar's estate prospered under Joseph's administration. A person with an unforgiving spirit nearly always seeks to exact some type of revenge—even if not on the person who caused him or her the original injury. It's a part of the unforgiving person's attempt to regain control after having felt humiliated and being without power. But Joseph didn't act in vengeance against Potiphar. He worked in such a way that Potiphar was blessed.

We know from Joseph's experience in Potiphar's house that he was a forgiving man because of these words: "The Lord blessed the Egyptian's house for Joseph's sake; and the blessing of the Lord was on all that he had in the house and in the field" (verse 5). God's anointing does not rest on people with an unforgiving spirit.

The events that immediately followed also reveal that Joseph had a forgiving spirit. One day, Joseph entered Potiphar's house and found himself alone with Potiphar's wife. She attempted to seduce him, but he refused her. She grabbed his outer garment as he attempted to escape, and he slipped out of his robe and left her holding it. Angry that she was rejected, Potiphar's wife used Joseph's garment as evidence in trumped-up charges of attempted rape. Potiphar had little recourse other than to commit Joseph to prison (see Genesis 39:7–20).

How does this illustrate a forgiving spirit in Joseph? A person who has been injured repeatedly in the past, and especially by those in authority in the immediate family (such as victims of physical and emotional abuse, sexual abuse, or incest), is prone to develop a victim syndrome. A pattern of victimization readily develops unless there is intervention in the person's life to restore a sense of self-esteem. This focus on victimization often goes hand in glove with unforgiveness. The person relives painful moments, and each time, the memories tear down the person and weaken self-esteem and courage. Ultimately, the person has little inner strength or power to resist the advances of any person who attempts to use or abuse him further—especially a person who is perceived to be in authority.

Joseph exhibited *none* of this syndrome. He had no perception of himself as a victim. He operated in strength and conviction in rejecting Potiphar's wife.

3. "[Joseph] refused and said to [Potiphar's] wife, 'Look, my master does not know what is with me in the house, and he has committed all that he has to my hand. There is no one greater in this house than I, nor has he kept back anything from me but you, because you are his wife. How then can I do this great wickedness, and sin against God?'" (Genesis 39:8–9). What were Joseph's reasons for refusing Potiphar's wife?

4. Joseph showed gratitude toward both Potiphar and God. What does this reveal about the process of forgiving others?

Joseph in Prison

In prison, we read that Joseph rose to leadership, which reveals the experience with Potiphar's wife did not leave him with a spirit of unforgiveness. Once again, Joseph proved himself worthy of trust. The keeper of the prison turned over all the administration of the prison to Joseph, including supervision of the other prisoners. Again, this is clear evidence that Joseph had not developed an angry, bitter, resentful attitude (see Genesis 39:21–23).

In prison, a butler shared a dream with Joseph, which the Lord enabled him to interpret. Joseph told the butler he would be restored to his position as Pharaoh's cupbearer. Then he said to him, "Remember me when it is well with you, and please show kindness to me; make mention of me to Pharaoh, and get me out of this house [prison]. For indeed I was stolen away from the land of the Hebrews; and also I have done nothing here that they should put me into the dungeon" (40:14–15).

The butler was restored as Joseph foretold, but he neglected to mention Joseph for two full years. Two years is a long time to be forgotten in prison. Bitterness and unforgiveness can take root during that time. How do we know this didn't happen in Joseph's life? Because the day came when the butler *remembered* Joseph.

Pharaoh had two troubling dreams, and none of his magicians or wise men could interpret them. So Joseph was called from prison and brought before Pharaoh. Pharaoh told Joseph his dreams, and with God's help, he interpreted them. Then Joseph gave God's advice to Pharaoh for responding to the situation foretold in the dreams.

A person with an unforgiving spirit usually can't wait to tell the story of his injuries. He is eager to elicit support, sympathy, or justice. Yet Joseph made no appeals on his own behalf during his meeting with Pharaoh. Even when Pharaoh elevated Joseph to a high position, he made no request for justice on his own behalf.

It was as if Joseph had forgotten all that had happened to him. He had forgiven the failures and sins of others against him and had moved forward into success in his leadership role. Under Joseph, a plan was put into place that was for the blessing of Egypt and the preservation of people. Joseph was not a man motivated by vengeance.

5. "Yet the chief butler did not remember Joseph, but forgot him" (Genesis 40:23). When have you been forgotten by someone who could have helped you? Did you allow resentment to build toward that person? How did you deal with that resentment?

6. "Beware that you do not forget the Lord your God by not keeping His commandments, His judgments, and His statutes which I command you today" (Deuteronomy 8:11). What are some ways that we "forget" the Lord our God? What does this say about not harboring resentment toward others who forget us?

JOSEPH CONFRONTS HIS BROTHERS

The day came when a famine covered the land and Joseph's brothers had to travele to Egypt to buy food. Joseph at last came face to face with the brothers who had sold him into slavery so many years before. They didn't recognize him, but he recognized them. Yet there was no unforgiveness in the way he dealt with them. In revealing his identity to them, Joseph said:

> I am Joseph your brother, whom you sold into Egypt. But now, do not therefore be grieved or angry with yourselves because you sold me here; for God sent me before you to preserve life. For these two years the famine has been in the land, and there are still five years in which there will be neither plowing nor harvesting. And God sent me before you to preserve a posterity for you in the earth, and to save your lives by a great deliverance. So now it was not you who sent me here, but God; and He has made me a father to Pharaoh, and lord of all his house, and a ruler throughout all the land of Egypt.
>
> Hurry and go up to my father, and say to him, "Thus says your son Joseph: 'God has made me lord of all Egypt; come down to me, do not tarry. You shall dwell in the land of Goshen, and you shall be near to me, you and your children, your children's children, your flocks and your herds, and all that you have. There I will provide for you, lest you and your household, and all that you have, come to poverty; for there are still five years of famine.'" . . .
>
> You shall tell my father of all my glory in Egypt, and of all that you have seen; and you shall hurry and bring my father down here. Then he fell on his brother Benjamin's neck and wept, and Benjamin wept on his neck. Moreover he kissed all his brothers and wept over them (Genesis 45:4–9, 13–15).

The scene was permeated with forgiveness. The last thing a person with an unforgiving spirit does is seek the good of those who have hurt him. Yet rather than exact any vengeance or retribution on his brothers, Joseph responded to them with compassion, love, and provision. He wept with them. Above all, he saw God's higher purpose in all the events of his life.

7. According to Joseph, how did he arrive in Egypt? Where is his focus in all the events of his life?

8. How can this attitude speed the process of forgiving those who betray you?

The Key to a Forgiving Spirit

Joseph's story reveals the key to a forgiving spirit is to see *divine purpose* in any event that happens to us. God has a plan and purpose for us, and He does not allow adversity to come into our lives without a specific reason that can eventually work for our good. Joseph was able to see an ultimate purpose for all that had happened to him. As he later said to his brothers:

> Do not be afraid, for am I in the place of God? But as for you, you meant evil against me; but God meant it for good, in order to bring it about as it is this day, to save many people alive. Now therefore, do not be afraid; I will provide for you and your little ones (Genesis 50:19–21).

Joseph saw God's hand in allowing him to be brought to Egypt. He saw God's hand in giving him experience after experience in which he could grow in leadership skills and understand the ways of the Egyptians. He saw how God protected him and prepared him through the years.

When you can look at any hurtful experience that comes your way and say, "God has a purpose in this," you are on your way to developing a forgiving spirit. God *does* have a purpose. It may be to do a work in the life of the person who wronged you. It may be to perfect an area of your life. It may be to make you stronger. It may be to train you to have a forgiving spirit!

Whatever God's reasons are for you to feel pain or suffer at the hands of others, the outcome for you can be good—but only if you are willing to forgive those who hurt you.

How Many Times Are We to Forgive?

Joseph was repeatedly called on to forgive those who had wronged him, which raises the question as to how many times we are to forgive. In the New Testament, we read how Peter one day approached Jesus and asked this very question: "Lord, how often shall my brother sin against me, and I forgive him? Up to seven times?" Peter no doubt thought he was being generous in citing seven times. But Jesus said to Peter, "I do not say to you, up to seven times, but up to seventy times seven" (Matthew 18:21–22).

We are to forgive immediately *and continually*, and to forgive all who hurt us. There never comes a time when we can say to an offending person, "You've crossed the line." Our forgiveness is to know no limit. Joseph certainly never reached a limit in his ability to forgive others—and neither did Jesus. He extended forgiveness repeatedly during His lifetime. Even as He hung on the cross, He forgave those who had put Him there, saying, "Father, forgive them, for they do not know what they do" (Luke 23:34). We must follow their example.

9. "Joseph said to them, 'Do not be afraid, for am I in the place of God?' But as for you, you meant evil against me; but God meant it for good, in order to bring it about as it is this day, to save many people alive" (Genesis 50:19–20). What did Joseph mean by asking his brothers if he was "in the place of God"? What does this suggest about taking revenge?

10. Why did Joseph forgive his brothers? How did his focus on God's sovereignty help him to forgive?

TODAY AND TOMORROW

Today: Joseph viewed everything as part of God's plan for his life, and therefore he could forgive others quickly.

Tomorrow: I will ask the Lord to help me see how He is leading all events in my life.

CLOSING PRAYER

Lord God, there are so many reasons we can have to develop an unforgiving spirit, but lead us to follow the example of Joseph—and Your Son—and live in such a way that we let go of our bitterness and embrace the plans that You have for us. Thank You, Father, that Jesus said that He had come to set the captives free—to liberate those in bondage. We pray that the Holy Spirit will take this message on forgiveness that we have received today and drive it home so that it will stick in our lives, so there will be fruit in abundance. Help us to truly understand and accept that You can bring good out of any situation, no matter how painful it seems. Amen.

Notes and Prayer Requests

Use this space to write any key points, questions, or prayer requests from this week's study.

LESSON 10

The Challenge of Forgiving Ourselves

IN THIS LESSON

Learning: But what if I can't forgive myself?

Growing: How can I get out from under this burden of guilt and shame?

Our heavenly Father wants us to experience *complete* forgiveness. He wants to forgive our sins through the atonement of Jesus on the cross. For this reason, confessing, repenting, and coming to the Father to ask for forgiveness should be as natural to us as breathing air into our lungs. By doing these things, we can maintain our fellowship with God and enjoy the many benefits of His intimate presence.

As we have seen, God cannot use us for His purposes on this earth if we are harboring sin in our lives or if we are harboring an unforgiving spirit. He wants to remove the barriers to His blessings—our pride, our false sense of humility, our false guilt, and our unconfessed sin. As Paul wrote, "Therefore, as the elect of God, holy and beloved, put on tender mercies, kindness, humility, meekness, longsuffering; bearing with one another, and forgiving one another, if anyone has a complaint against another; even as Christ forgave you" (Colossians 3:12–13).

We are to forgive others as Jesus has forgiven us. But sometimes, as we will discuss in this lesson, the most difficult person to forgive is the *one you face in the mirror*. God's Word is clear, however, that forgiveness is not complete until you *forgive yourself*.

Biblical Examples of Self-Forgiveness

If anybody had reason not to forgive himself, it was Peter. On what must have been the most demanding night of Jesus' life, Peter denied that he knew his Master. Jesus had foretold Peter's behavior, saying, "Assuredly, I say to you that this night, before the rooster crows, you will deny Me three times" (Matthew 26:34). Sure enough, Peter did.

We don't know how Peter might have cried out to his heavenly Father in the aftermath of what he did that night. We don't know what Peter might have said to the Lord after Jesus' resurrection. But we do know this: Peter trusted Jesus to forgive what he had done. And Jesus trusted Peter to receive forgiveness.

After Jesus rose from the dead, an angel said to the women who came to the tomb, "Go, tell His disciples—and Peter—that He is going before you into Galilee" (Mark 16:7). Jesus *expected* Peter to continue to follow Him. And Peter did. Later, Jesus met Peter and some of the disciples by the shore of the Sea of Galilee. Peter heard the Lord's voice calling from the shore, and he left his fishing boat and "plunged into the sea" (John 21:7). He was in a hurry to get to Jesus as fast as he could! This is the response of a person who feels fully forgiven.

Jesus asked Peter three times, "Do you love Me?" Three times, Peter said, "Yes, Lord; You know that I love You." Three times, Jesus commanded Peter to care for the lambs and sheep of His flock. At the close of Jesus' conversation with Peter, He said to him the same words He said at the beginning of their relationship: "Follow Me" (John 21:15-19). Peter had a second chance to be Jesus' disciple, and he took the opportunity for full restoration.

Peter became a vigorous leader in the early church. His sermon on the Feast of Pentecost was one of the most effective and powerful soul-winning sermons ever preached. He could never have preached such sermons or enjoyed such anointing on his life if he had not first been able to receive God's forgiveness for himself. God does not anoint a spirit of unforgiveness—even if the person that you are refusing to forgive is yourself.

Paul also was able to forgive himself. He referred to himself as the chief of all sinners—and this may very well have been the case. Yet no one preached forgiveness more than Paul. Paul declared, "This is a faithful saying and worthy of all acceptance, that Christ Jesus came into the world to save sinners" (1 Timothy 1:15). No matter what you may have done, you have not "outsinned" Peter and Paul. They received God's *complete* forgiveness, including the ability to forgive themselves—and so can you.

1. "If we are faithless, He remains faithful; He cannot deny Himself" (2 Timothy 2:13). When have you been faithless to God? In what way is any sin an act of faithlessness toward God?

2. What does it mean that God "cannot deny Himself"? How is it an act of denying God's grace when you won't forgive yourself?

Reasons Why We Don't Forgive Ourselves

There are number of reasons why we may choose not to forgive ourselves. *First, we may not have really experienced God's forgiveness.* We cannot forgive ourselves until we first know in our hearts, and accept fully by faith, that God can and does forgive us.

Second, we think we know something about our sin God doesn't know—and we assume God wouldn't forgive us if He knew the full details. Is there something about the facts, consequences, or motivations of our sin that we believe is hidden from God? Let me assure you, He knows all about what we have done and who we are. He knows our thoughts and motives (see 1 Corinthians 3:20). He sees it all.

Third, we are performance-based. We tend to create our own self-identities on the basis of things we have accomplished more than the inner qualities we are developing. Sin is part of our performance, and we feel a need to work to remedy a bad showing and turn our evil deeds into something that can be placed in the "win" column. God does not forgive us, however, on the basis of our performance. He forgives us because it is His gracious will to forgive.

Fourth, we don't know how to deal with self-disappointment. To be disappointed in people, we must first expect them to do something that they cannot or will not do. God doesn't expect us to go through life without failures and sins. Therefore, God isn't surprised by our failures, and He is not disappointed. God doesn't expect us to come to Him with a report of perfect living, but He does expect us to come to Him in our sin and ask for His forgiveness.

Fifth, we emotionally adjust to the guilt. At some point, we emotionally adjust to feeling guilty, and we find we are afraid to be free of our guilt because it has become so much a part of our self-identity. If we find this has become our mindset, we need to ask God to give us the courage to forgive ourselves and lead a guilt-free life.

Sixth, we consider ourselves to be exempt or different from other people. We believe there are "extenuating circumstances" regarding our situation that places them above God's Word. This simply isn't the case. The Bible tells us, "God shows no partiality. But in every nation whoever fears Him and works righteousness is accepted by Him" (Acts 10:34–35). God makes the forgiveness He gives available to all.

Seventh, we expect to sin again. We reason, therefore ,that we can't forgive ourselves because we know we are weak and are bound to fail again in the future. Of course, God knows this as well. Nevertheless, He invites us to come to Him for forgiveness.

Eighth, we are confronted by the consequences of our sin and draw a conclusion we can't be fully forgiven. Sometimes we see the consequences of our sin in someone else's life. We chastise ourselves when we see that person struggle and feel the weight of our sin once again. Or perhaps that outward sign is in our own lives. We may be in prison for what we have done, so we don't see how we can be forgiven and freed from our sin while the images of bondage are all around us. In such cases, we need to recognize we are being held captive in our hearts. But Jesus came to set the captives free (see Luke 4:18). We can't keep ourselves captive when He has given us the keys to our prison cell.

Ninth, we have low self-esteem. We may have such low self-esteem that we can't imagine anything good being done for us. We are reluctant to accept what Jesus did and have little ability to do something good for ourselves—including forgiving ourselves. In such a situation, we need to read the many promises God has given us in the Scriptures—and *then believe they are true.* We are His beloved children.

Tenth, we have a secret fear we might get away with our sin when we know we need to be punished. Most of us are raised in homes where we receive punishment of some type for the wrongs we do. We don't feel right if we do something wrong and suffer no consequences for it. But let me assure you, *all* sin has its consequences. The Lord may or may not ease the consequences of our sin. We may commit a terrible crime, receive God's forgiveness, and still spend many years in prison. We may sin in a way that causes physical damage to our body, receive God's forgiveness, and still suffer in our body. Even if we think we are getting away with sin, the truth is we are not. Sin will eventually manifest itself in consequences.

In receiving God's forgiveness and forgiving ourselves, we are not absolving ourselves of consequences. We are restoring our relationship with our heavenly Father and putting ourselves in a position to receive the help of the Holy Spirit in dealing with the consequences.

3. "There is therefore now no condemnation to those who are in Christ Jesus, who do not walk according to the flesh, but according to the Spirit" (Romans 8:1). What does it mean to "walk according to the flesh"? To walk "according to the Spirit"?

4. If God has no condemnation for you, what right do you have to condemn yourself? What role are you playing if you do so?

The Problem of False Guilt

As we discussed in an earlier lesson, there may be times when we find it difficult to forgive ourselves for something that happened in our lives, even though we haven't sinned before God. Accidents happen. We fail and make mistakes. Not all errors are sins before God. Not all bad things require God's forgiveness.

For example, consider the case of a man who is driving down the street and a toddler rushes into the path of his car. He isn't speeding. He applies the brakes immediately. Still, his car strikes and seriously injures the child. The man feels great sorrow and remorse, and for years, he is unable to forgive himself for what happened. This man is suffering false guilt. He has not sinned. He needs to ask God to restore his joy and then accept, by faith, that God will heal him and make him whole. This isn't a matter of sin and forgiveness.

Or consider the woman who goes through a divorce she did not want. She did everything in her ability to keep the marriage together, but her husband willfully abandons her and her children. The woman finds it difficult to forgive herself for the divorce and its effects on her children. This woman, too, is suffering false guilt. She has not sinned. She, too, needs to go to God and ask for a healing of her broken heart, and then to believe with faith that God will heal her.

False guilt can keep us in a prison just as surely as can refusing to forgive ourselves. We need to recognize false guilt for what it is and rely on God to heal us from the pain.

5. When have you suffered from false guilt? What effect did it have on your life? On your relationships with others and with God?

6. How do you determine whether guilt is false or justified? What role is played by prayer? By wise counsel? By God's Word?

Seven Questions to Ask Ourselves

A failure to forgive yourself will have the same consequences as a failure to forgive others. You will experience emotional bondage, uneasiness in your spirit, and a cloud of uncertainty about your relationship with God. You will find it difficult to relate to others, and your ability to minister or witness about God's love will be diminished. You may suffer physical damage in your body from the stress of unforgiven sin. You are likely to have your self-respect damaged and your self-esteem diminished. You may develop a false sense of humility.

There are no good results from a failure to forgive yourself. There are only negative by-products. For this reason, if you find that you are struggling today with forgiving yourself, I encourage you to ask yourself the following seven questions.

First, why should you continue to condemn yourself when God no longer condemns you? God has forgiven you. On what basis do you have grounds to override His forgiveness?

Second, is your self-condemnation drawing you into a more intimate relationship with God? The truth is that it cannot.

Third, what good are you doing to yourself or others by continually condemning yourself? Nothing good comes from self-condemnation.

Fourth, is your unwillingness to forgive yourself helping you build relationships? You may be building relationships, but they cannot be healthy ones.

Fifth, is your self-condemnation influencing God? In other words, is God going to be impressed with your lack of self-forgiveness? Is God going to do anything He would not do if you did forgive myself? The answer is no, on all accounts.

Sixth, is there any scriptural basis for continuing to condemn yourself? No, there is scriptural evidence for your not continuing to do so (see Romans 8:1).

Seventh, how long do you intend to condemn yourself? How much self-condemnation is enough? How many years of self-unforgiveness suffice? The time to forgive yourself is *now*!

7. "Most assuredly, I say to you, whoever commits sin is a slave of sin. And a slave does not abide in the house forever, but a son abides forever. Therefore if the Son makes you free, you shall be free indeed" (John 8:34–36). In what ways does God's forgiveness set you free? How does self-condemnation make you a slave to sin?

8. "Come to Me, all you who labor and are heavy laden, and I will give you rest" (Matthew 11:28). What burdens of unforgiveness are weighing you down? What will you do to get free of them?

The Steps to Self-Forgiveness

The steps to self-forgiveness are the same as those in forgiving others. *First, make an honest confession of the specific wrongs that you have committed.* Admit to God, "I'm guilty."

Second, confess that you have been harboring unforgiveness against yourself. Confess to God, "I have kept myself in emotional bondage over this. I know it's wrong. I repent of it and ask You to forgive me for doing this to myself."

Third, reaffirm your faith in God's promises of forgiveness. Speak aloud the verses that affirm your salvation (see, for example, John 3:16, Romans 10:9–10, and 1 John 1:9). Act on your faith and out of your will, saying, "God, on the basis of Your forgiveness, I now release myself from all guilt and condemnation. I accept Your forgiveness, and I forgive myself. I declare myself to be *completely* free of this sin, guilt, and shame because of Christ's work in me."

Finally, ask God to help you to walk with boldness and courage—and to leave all responsibility for your sin behind you at the cross.

9. "He has not dealt with us according to our sins, nor punished us according to our iniquities. For as the heavens are high above the earth, so great is His mercy toward those who fear Him; as far as the east is from the west, so far has He removed our transgressions from us" (Psalm 103:10–12). How high are "the heavens" above the earth? How great is God's mercy toward you?

10. If you travel north to south, you will eventually start moving back north again—but this is not possible when traveling east to west. What does this reveal about how far God has removed your sins?

TODAY AND TOMORROW

Today: God has already forgiven me, and I have no right to condemn myself.

Tomorrow: I will ask the Lord to set me free of my burden of guilt and shame.

Closing Prayer

Heavenly Father, so many of us are hurting so badly today because we are filled with guilt over the wrongs we have done. Our minds and our spirits are clouded with guilt, and we feel trodden down, beaten down, and so unworthy to be called Your children. We wonder if You truly love us and we fear within our hears that we will never be able to match up to Your expectations. Today, we ask that You would help us accept that through our confession, repentance, and faith, You promise to accept us, receive us, and restore us into fellowship with You. Thank You, Lord, that we are never "too far gone" to experience the blood-bought forgiveness purchased at Calvary. Allow us to lead a life honorable of that cross. In Jesus' name we pray. Amen.

Notes and Prayer Requests

Use this space to write any key points, questions, or prayer requests from this week's study.

LESSON 11

When a Fellow Christian Stumbles

IN THIS LESSON

Learning: How should I respond when fellow believers are ensnared in sin?

Growing: What steps can I take to help fellow believers experience spiritual restoration through God's grace?

There are truly few forces in the universe more powerful than forgiveness. Forgiveness changes our behavior. It changes our lives. In the Gospels, we see how on the cross at Calvary, a single act of forgiveness changed the course of human history for thousands of years—and will continue to change it for thousands upon thousands more.

In previous lessons, we have seen that forgiveness is a cornerstone of the Christian faith. We have seen that forgiveness is a matter of life and death. We have explored how to forgive others and how to forgive ourselves, and we have highlighted the corrosive danger of unforgiveness in our lives.

Now, in this final lesson, it is time to look at the critical role of forgiveness in the restoration of our fellow brothers and sisters in Christ when they fall into sin. Specifically, we will explore three truths that should govern our behavior in such circumstances: (1) every believer is subject to stumbling, (2) we have a responsibility to restore a brother or sister in Christ who falls into sin—no matter what, and (3) there are several important steps a believer needs to walk through in order to experience that restoration.

1. When were you impacted in a major way by the failure of someone you admire? How did you respond to that situation?

2. Why do you think it is often difficult to confront another believer in Christ when he or she has fallen into sin?

Every Believer Can Stumble

Let's start things off by looking at the wisdom of God's Word. In Galatians 6:1–5, the apostle Paul writes, "Brethren, if a man is overtaken in any trespass, you who are spiritual restore such a one in a spirit of gentleness, considering yourself lest you also be tempted.

Bear one another's burdens, and so fulfill the law of Christ. For if anyone thinks himself to be something, when he is nothing, he deceives himself. But let each one examine his own work, and then he will have rejoicing in himself alone, and not in another. For each one shall bear his own load."

The first truth we need to remember regarding the forgiveness and restoration of fellow believers is that every believer—every single disciple of Jesus—is subject to stumbling. Every Christian (and that includes you and me) is vulnerable to falling into sin, even after they have experienced salvation and transformation through Christ. We know this to be true. We have seen the evidence in our own lives. But why is it true?

The Bible says all of us have the old sin nature still within us. No matter how committed we are to Jesus Christ, no matter how well we understand what it means to be filled with the Holy Spirit, there is still within us that predilection or that natural inclination to sin. Some people call it our "sin nature." Paul describes it in Romans 7:19 when he says, "For the good that *I will to do*, I do not do; but the evil *I will not to do*, that I practice" (emphasis added).

Another reason we still struggle with sin is that we have an enemy who is called the "prince of the powers of the air" (Ephesians 2:2). Satan is always there to harass us, to tempt us, to put pressure on us, and to do whatever else he can to try and cause us to fail. So, we see that we have an enemy on the inside, which is the old pattern of sin. And we have an enemy on the outside, which is Satan.

And, of course, we can add a third reason why all Christians are vulnerable to sin, which is our world system with all its allurements and temptations. In many ways, it's easier to stumble into sin today than it has ever been before.

There is an insight to be found in that idea of "stumbling," or of being caught or surprised. This is the concept that Paul was exploring in Galatians 6:1 when he wrote, "If any man is overtaken in any trespass . . ." The word translated *trespass* carries the meaning of a blunder or fault. That is, we are not necessarily talking about a willful sin where people plot out something they are going to do in rebellion against God. Instead, this is a moment of weakness. There is a sudden pressure, perhaps a sudden temptation, and then quickly a fall.

It happens. And it can happen to any of us . . . even as followers of Christ. It is important to remember this truth because you will be much more eager to forgive a fellow Christian who stumbles into sin when you are fully aware of your own vulnerability to sin. You will be much more willing to do the work involved in restoring that fellow brother or sister in Christ—and we'll explore that work in greater detail below—when you remember that you might be in need of such restoration in days to come.

3. "Therefore let him who thinks he stands take heed lest he fall" (1 Corinthians 10:12). Why it is important to remember that each of us can fall into sin? What is the danger of thinking that you are strong against a particular temptation?

4. When were you impacted in a major way by the failure of someone you admire? How did you respond to that situation?

5. What are some of the factors in our society and in the church today that make it easier for Christians to stumble?

OUR RESPONSIBILITY TO RESTOR BELIEVERS WHO STUMBLE

The second truth we need to remember is that all Christians have a definite responsibility to restore a fellow believer who has fallen into sin. Look again at what Paul wrote to the Galatians: "Brethren, if a man is overtaken in any trespass, you who are spiritual restore such a one in a spirit of gentleness, considering yourself lest you also be tempted" (6:1).

Once again, this is a command. It's not a suggestion. It's not even a strongly worded recommendation. This is a direct command given to the church by God through Paul, who was writing under the inspiration of the Holy Spirit. In other words, we need to take this verse seriously. We need to take this charge seriously.

There are many Christians today who shy away from the work of spiritual restoration because they don't want to get their hands dirty. Or they are worried about somehow being viewed as guilty by association. "I don't want to get myself mixed up in that situation." But Paul said "you who are spiritual" are to restore the person.

Notice that Paul didn't put any conditions on the command. He didn't say to think about restoring your brothers or sisters who have sinned after you have examined the situation to find out whether they are really guilty. He didn't say to wait until they have suffered long enough or until you think they have paid for their sins. This is instant. It's an immediate responsibility.

Look at the word *restore* in Galatians 6:1. In the original Greek, this term was used for a physician who reset the bones of a broken limb. It carries the idea of putting things back the way they belong. It's making things right again–making it so everything fits in the proper place again. I like the way that sounds. I want to be part of that kind of work, because I know how it feels when I've been distorted or bent out of shape because of sin. As disciples of Jesus, we have the chance to participate in restoring others to their right positions–to be a vehicle through which someone is spiritually mended once again. This is a great privilege.

Look also at the word *spiritual*. As in, "You who are spiritual restore such a one." What does that mean? Are we talking about someone who is especially pious? Someone who always chooses to go to church instead of watching a ballgame? No, according to the Scripture, a spiritual person is simply one who has received the Lord Jesus Christ as their Savior. It is a person who is walking in the Spirit, living out of the Spirit, and responding to life through the Spirit of God who is within them. Does that describe you?

This is a person who is walking in the Spirit to care for others and offer love, forgiveness, encouragement, and acceptance. This is a person who reaches out to others without condemnation or judgment, but instead embraces others just the way they are. And that is critical, because it is so easy for us as Christians to place ourselves in judgment over others. It is especially easy for us to place ourselves above those who are visibly and perhaps publicly struggling with sin.

This must not be true of us as belivers in Christ Jesus, because judgment has no place in a heart ready to do the work of forgiveness. Condemnation has no place in a soul ready to join the important, life-giving work of restoration. "You who are spiritual restore such a one in a spirit of gentleness."

6. "Brethren, if a man is overtaken in any trespass, you who are spiritual restore such a one in a spirit of gentleness, considering yourself lest you also be tempted" (Galatians 6:1). What does it mean to consider yourself "lest you also be tempted"?

7. What obstacles might hinder you from actively seeking to restore a fellow believer caught in sin?

8. Based on the definition offered above, would you consider yourself "spiritual"? Explain.

Walking Toward Restoration

When someone in your life or in your sphere of influence has stumbled spiritually, you have a command from God to extend forgiveness and grace to that person, because you know you are vulnerable to the same trap. The same failure. In addition, you are responsible to help restore that person to a proper fellowship with God.

You're probably wondering, "How? How do I participate in the spiritual restoration of other believers?" I am glad you asked! There are six steps in the process, so let's run through them one at a time.

First, help them recognize their failure. Don't make excuses. Don't pretend everything is okay. Lead them toward the truth: they have been ensnared by sin, which always comes with consequences. Help them recognize their situation.

Second, lead them to acknowledge responsibility for their sin. Don't let them blame it on somebody else—and especially don't let them blame it on you. Yes, it's true that others may have contributed to their sinful patterns, and there may even be those who pushed them toward sin. But in the end, the choices were up to them and no other. So, as you walk with these believers toward spiritual restoration, help them take responsibility for their sin.

Third, lead them to repent of their sin, which also includes confession. Guide them to vocally confess their sin to God—to speak it aloud. But also guide them to repent, which means to have a change of mind that leads to a change of attitude that leads to a change in behavior. Remember that this is the key. Repentance always carries with it a change of direction—you were going one direction, but now you turn around 180 degrees. You change your direction and walk away from your sin and back toward God. When done correctly, this confession and this repentance should carry a sense of remorse and regret. The individuals should feel the weight of their rebellion against a just and holy God.

Fourth, lead them to restitution. Note that this may only apply in some cases. If the person you are working with stole something, for example, he or she needs to pay it back. The person needs to make restitution. If that person treated someone shamefully or abusively, there needs to be some effort given to make things right. "I know that I hurt you, and I know you probably don't want to hear anything from me right now. But I want to say I'm sorry, and I want to do whatever I can to restore what I took from you."

Fifth, help them receive the message God is sending through their failure. If that sounds strange, remember that God is all-knowing. He does not waste any opportunity to speak with us and lead us to grow toward holiness—even the opportunities presented by our failures. Remember also that God *allowed* the failure to take place. He could have stopped it. He could have prevented the snare or the trap or whatever seduced this person into sin. But He did not. Often, that is because He has a message He wants to send.

Notice that I didn't say God *caused* the failure. I didn't say God *tempted* anyone to fail. Scripture makes it clear that God does not tempt us to sin in any way (see James 1:13). But God does use those moments after we give in to temptation. So help the person seeking restoration to examine his or her failure and discover what God wants to teach through it.

Sixth, lead them to respond to God's chastisement with gratitude. This may be the most difficult step of all. In Psalm 119, David offered a good basis for this step when he wrote, "Before I was afflicted I went astray, But now I keep Your word" (verse 67). He also states, "It is good for me that I have been afflicted, That I may learn Your statutes. The law of Your mouth is better to me Than thousands of coins of gold and silver" (verses 71–72).

David was able to express gratitude to God for the discipline he received—for the way he was "afflicted." And God still offers discipline and chastisement to His children today. When we rebel against Him, He forgives us and loves us, but He also disciplines us. He also corrects us, often through the natural consequences of our sin. Therefore, as you help others walk toward spiritual restoration, lead them to accept God's discipline. Help them to not only accept it but also be grateful for His work in their lives through that discipline.

Seventh, when you approach a brother or sister in Christ who has stumbled, do so in a spirit of gentleness. Remember this is a *person* who is hurting. This is a person for whom Christ died. Therefore, approach that individual in a spirit of gentleness and humility, recognizing you could easily be in his or her shoes. Yes, you want to help the person recognize the sin. Yes, you want to help the person assume responsibility for that sin. And yes, you want to lead them to make restitution, receive God's message, and accept God's discipline with gratitude. But you can accomplish all of that in gentleness and humility. Not in judgment or condemnation.

When you receive and experience God's forgiveness—and extend that forgiveness to your fellow believers in Christ—you will be made whole in your humanity, even as you are prepared for ministry in His kingdom and for life everlasting. So choose to experience God's complete forgiveness in your life, and also choose to help others experience the joy of that same experience. You can do it in this very hour.

9. What are some obstacles that might hinder you from walking with someone through these steps toward restoration?

10. What steps can you take right now to prepare yourself to overcome those obstacles?

TODAY AND TOMORROW

Today: God will empower me to participate in His work of spiritual restoration.

Tomorrow: I will ask the Holy Spirit this week to show me how I can join Him in leading others toward restoration.

CLOSING PRAYER

Heavenly Father, we know that even those who have put their trust in You will fail us at times. We know that we ourselves will fail our fellow brothers and sisters in Christ at times. Thank You that You have made a way for us to find forgiveness and love one another with the supernatural love that only You can provide. Today, we pray that many people would come to You for salvation. We pray they would experience the freedom that trusting in Christ provides—freedom from living under a cloud of guilt, freedom from the pain that has driven them to seek retribution against others, and freedom from the quest to continually "perform" in order to somehow achieve Your approval. Let them know that You love them and accept them. Bring them to confession, repentance, and salvation. In Your name we pray. Amen.

Notes and Prayer Requests

Use this space to write any key points, questions, or prayer requests from this week's study.

LESSON 12

Reviewing the Key Principles

IN THIS LESSON

Learning: Why is unforgiveness such a dangerous presence?

Growing: What steps can I take to deal with unforgiveness?

It's possible that in spite of the insights you have gained so far, there is still one event you haven't yet released or resolved. Someone hurt you, and your first response was to retaliate because you felt like you had the right to exact a little revenge. But then outwardly you decided not to retaliate, because you are a Christian and you are supposed to "be nice." So you said nothing . . . and you did nothing.

Was that the end of the story? No, because that hurt you felt did not go away. You just stuffed it down, and it's been sitting there inside you ever since. Also, maybe you saw that same person again, or maybe several times recently. And the hurt and the desire to retaliate got bigger each time, but you stuffed it all down again. But the truth is that it's all still there. And it's killing you.

In this study, we've seen the power of forgiveness both in us and through us. In this final lesson, we will review the main principles we've covered and take a last look at the other side. Because whether we know it or not, there's little in our lives more dangerous than a spirit of unforgiveness—and we need to secure the victory over it.

1. "You have heard that it was said, 'An eye for an eye and a tooth for a tooth. But I tell you not to resist an evil person. But whoever slaps you on your right cheek, turn the other to him also'" (Matthew 5:38–39). How does Jesus say to respond to a person who treats you badly? What does this say about exacting revenge ?

2. When are some times you have been tempted to retaliate against a person who wronged you? What was the result of your actions?

The Danger of Unforgiveness

Maybe right now you're still wondering, "What's the big deal? Sure, something happened a while back, but I've forgotten all about it.

It's all water under the bridge." I wish that were the case. I really do. In fact, it may be true you've forgotten about it in your mind, and it may be true that you believe everything is over and done with. But the reality is that your body and your heart are still being affected by unforgiveness because of what you stuffed down inside you.

You simply cannot escape the consequences of an unforgiving spirit—because it's so subtle. Deep down inside, your unforgiveness is still boiling away. The acid is still working away. And it's going to keep working away at you until you do something to deal with it.

Again, you might be thinking, "But I don't feel anything! If unforgiveness really was so bad, wouldn't I feel it?" Well, a person can have cancer for years without feeling it. A person can have heart trouble for a long time before it manifests itself with any outward effects. There are a lot of things that can go on in the human body before you even know about it—and the same is true with the human spirit.

Just as important, unforgiveness is a disastrous attitude because it's a totally ungodly attitude. In fact, it's an attitude of rebellion against God. You can better understand God's opinion of unforgiveness when you look at it from the viewpoint of the cross. What did God accomplish at the cross? He paid the sin debt for every single person in the world, from Adam all the way to the last person to be born. That was the love of God. And He didn't put conditions on that act—He didn't forgive those who deserved it.

Instead, His awesome gift of forgiveness is offered to all.

3. How have you experienced the consequences of unforgiveness in your life?

4. How does unforgiveness represent a "rebellion" against God?

Unforgiveness Doesn't Fit

Again, unforgiveness is deliberate refusal on our part to give up our resentment about a wrong committed against us. It is a refusal to give up the right to get even, based on the attitude the other person needs to *pay* for the wrong that was done. That's really the key: as long as we feel someone has to pay, we are not walking in forgiveness. We have an attitude of unforgiveness. Why? Because the Lord says vengeance belongs to Him and Him alone (see Romans 12:19).

We often think, "That's not fair, because so-and-do got away with it!" But did the person *really* get away with it? Do you think anyone can get away with wrongdoing in the presence of God? No, it is not possible. God knows exactly how to take care of things—which is exactly why vengeance belongs only to Him.

Let's turn to God's Word to shine a light on the danger of unforgiveness. We will start with Ephesians 4:31–32: "Let all bitterness, wrath, anger, clamor, and evil speaking be put away from you, with all malice. And be kind to one another, tenderhearted, forgiving one another, even as God in Christ forgave you." The first thing to notice about these verses is that they are a command from the Lord. It's not optional. We are directly commanded to put away bitterness, wrath, anger—everything that leads to unforgiveness in our hearts. And we are to not only operate with kindness and tenderness but also with forgiveness—even as God has forgiven us through Christ.

This is the key. As followers of Jesus, it is never excusable for us to have an unforgiving spirit toward anyone, because when we accepted Christ as our Savior, we surrendered that right. We surrendered our lives to Him. And He has commanded us to forgive.

One way to think about it is like a suit of clothes. I wear a size 41 long. So, if I were to show up to church wearing a size 62 short, people would notice. They would tell me I need to go back home and change, because what I'm wearing doesn't fit. In the same way, unforgiveness does not "fit" you as a follower of Jesus. You can never make it fit you. It will always be out of place with your identity in Christ.

5. What does it mean to forgive "even as God in Christ forgave you"?

6. When was a time that you successfully "put away" anger or bitterness or evil?

Unforgiveness Hinders Our Spiritual Lives

Let's review another key Scripture on unforgiveness. This one comes from Jesus Himself: "And whenever you stand praying, if you have anything against anyone, forgive him, that your Father in heaven may also forgive you your trespasses. But if you do not forgive, neither will your Father in heaven forgive your trespasses" (Mark 11:25–26). Now, if that sounds serious to you—you're right. It's incredibly serious.

Maybe you're wondering, "Does that mean I lose my salvation because of unforgiveness?" No. When you and I trusted Jesus Christ as our personal Savior, we were pardoned from all of our sins and from the penalty of our sin. So, our salvation is secure.

What Jesus was talking about in these verses isn't our relationship with God but our fellowship with Him. When we refuse to forgive, we break that fellowship because we align ourselves against God and His will. We put ourselves in a place of rebellion against Him.

In other words, we cannot walk closely with God and harbor unforgiveness, resentment, hostility, anger, or bitterness toward somebody else in our hearts. Those two things are not compatible. They are mutually exclusive. We can try to be spiritual in all kinds of ways, but the Word of God is either true or it's not—and the Word says that if we refuse to forgive others, we will no longer occupy a place of right fellowship with Him.

On a practical level, there are many different ways unforgiveness hinders our spiritual lives. For example, we cannot have a good prayer life and hold a bitter spirit or unforgiveness in our hearts. Why? Because when we come to God and say, "Lord, I just want to thank You for being so good to me, and I'm confessing my sins . . ."—do you think God doesn't see that behind all that is an unforgiving spirit?

Listen, if we allow unforgiveness into our lives, it means our prayer life is basically over until we deal with it. You say to yourself, "I'm getting along fine." No, you just *think* you are. But what you can't see is what is on the inside and what is happening to you there.

Worship is another example. Think about these great songs of our faith: "My Jesus I love thee, I know Thou art mine; for Thee all the follies of sin I resign." "Amazing grace, how sweet the sound that saved a wretch like me." "This world is not my home, I'm just a-passing through." Now, how can someone sing these kinds of songs with any sincerity and genuine feeling when they've got an unforgiving spirit in their hearts?

That is hypocrisy. It just doesn't work.

In the same way, what kind of witness can we have when we are holding on to unforgiveness? How can we possibly tell others about God's wonderful gift of forgiveness from sin when we are still refusing to refuse others for their sins against us?

Even something like our giving to God is affected by our spirit of unforgiveness. Jesus told His disciples that if they come to the altar to present an offering to God, and they remember someone is in conflict with them, they should leave their gift and go make things right with that person (see Matthew 5:23–24). That is how seriously God takes unforgiveness, because it blocks our spiritual growth.

7. "If someone says, 'I love God,' and hates his brother, he is a liar; for he who does not love his brother whom he has seen, how can he love God whom he has not seen?" (1 John 4:20). What is the connection between loving others and loving God?

8. What are some areas of your spiritual life that currently feel stuck or in neutral? What are you doing to move forward in these areas of your life?

A Final Word on Unforgiveness

I hope as you have gone through this study that you have seen how critical a problem unforgiveness can be for our spiritual lives. In this closing section, we will review the key progression of steps that each of us needs to take if we desire to move past unforgiveness and truly restore our fellowship with God.

First, we have to acknowledge the fact that unforgiveness is serious business. We can't deal with unforgiveness lightly because we are dealing with our relationship to Almighty God. This includes assuming responsibility for the unforgiveness in our hearts. We need to acknowledge it to have the victory over it: "God, I am bitter. I am resentful. I am hostile. I have an unforgiving spirit. I am guilty of holding a grudge. I am guilty of disobeying Your law because I was unwilling to forgive. I accept these things as true, Lord."

One of the reasons that people so seldomly move beyond unforgiveness is because they can't seem to get over what was done to them. They can't get over the pain and the heartache that others caused in their lives. Therefore, we have to look beyond the hurt and pain. We can't focus on ourselves if we're going to deal with unforgiveness. Remember, unforgiveness is an act of rebellion toward God. Therefore, we need to change our thinking if we want to stop rebelling. We won't deal with unforgiveness until we see it the way God sees it. As long as we can smooth it over in our minds, we will keep trying to live with it. And we will remain in our rebellion.

Second, we need to ask God to forgive us. "God, please forgive me. I'm guilty. I violated Your law. I rebelled against Your Spirit. I've hurt other people. Please remove this sin from me."

Third—and this is where things can get difficult—we have to ask God to enable us to forgive. When we have lived with pain and unforgiveness for a long time, it can be hard to lay it down. In fact, it's likely we won't be able to do it in our own strength. We have to ask the Spirit of God that dwells within us to enable us and empower us to let go.

Like so many things in our spiritual lives, this is a decision that doesn't have to be based on a feeling. Meaning, we don't have to feel positively toward that person. We don't have to want the best for that person—not at first. We can simply say, "God, I choose to lay down my unforgiveness. I choose to lay it down by Your grace and Your mercy and in Your strength." If we ask God to do that, will He do it? Even if we don't feel it in our heart? Absolutely. We don't even have to pray, "Lord, if it is Your will . . ." We already know that it *is* His will. Releasing unforgiveness is always His will.

Now, does that mean we won't ever think about it anymore? Does that mean the pain and the negative feelings will go away? No, not at first. Maybe not ever. But it does mean that when we start to think about it—the pain, the anger, the reasons we have to withhold forgiveness—we can simply choose again to let it go. If we grab hold of it again, we will give Satan a foothold in our heart, and that can start the whole cycle all over again. So we must lay it down. The unforgiveness doesn't fit, remember? It's not part of who we are anymore.

Next, if we want to fully deal with unforgiveness, we need to start praying for the other person. I'm not talking about curse-like prayers—"Lord, smite them and send down Your fire to consume them!" No, I mean we need to pray for their benefit. We need to pray for God to be at work in their hearts and their lives. Pray for them to be transformed.

Let's say, for example, somebody has hurt you for years and years. You begin to pray for that person and ask God to open his or her eyes. You ask God to soften the person's heart through the work of His Holy Spirit. Here is what happens: the center of your attention has shifted and is no longer on you and how you got hurt. Now the center of attention is back on God and His good work in the world.

Finally, we may need to go to the person who wronged us and be honest with him or her. We may need to say, "Here's what happened a little while ago, and here's why I was hurt by it. But I'm coming to you today because I've been holding unforgiveness in my heart. I've kept hold of anger and bitterness, and I need to ask you to forgive me for that."

Now, we don't always take this step. In fact, it's probably better *not* to take this step if the person involved has no idea what has been going on or if the relationship with the person is not a safe one. This is something to pray about. Ask God whether or not you need to speak with that person and then follow where He leads.

Always remember that *unforgiveness is dangerous*. It doesn't fit you as a child of God. It hinders your spiritual growth. So if you really want to get deal with it, you need to do whatever is necessary to secure the victory over it. You've got to lay it down.

As long as you hold unforgiveness in your heart, you will be chained up by it. You will be carrying around your own prison of bitterness and pain. But when you choose to lay it down through the power of God and through the work of His Holy Spirit, you will be free!

9. "Do not lie to one another, since you have put off the old man with his deeds" (Colossians 3:9). If God leads you to approach the person whom you struggle to forgive, why is it critical to be completely honest about how he or she hurt you?

10. Which of the steps outlined this section seems most difficult to take? Why are those steps so difficult?

TODAY AND TOMORROW

Today: Unforgiveness doesn't fit my identity as a child of God.

Tomorrow: I will take whatever steps are necessary to lay down my unforgiveness and be free.

Closing Prayer

Heavenly Father, help us today to admit the deep hurt we have experienced at the hands of others. Reveal to us any areas where we have stuffed down that hurt—areas where the wound has poisoned our souls and is destroying our lives. We know that such unforgiveness doesn't "fit" our identity as Your children, and we do not want it to have any place in our hearts. Thank You, Lord, that before the world was even designed You were creating a marvelous plan for bringing us into wholeness and fellowship with You. Thank You that we can place our trust in Christ and know that He will take our pain and deal with the injustices we have faced. Amen.

Notes and Prayer Requests

Use this space to write any key points, questions, or prayer requests from this week's study.

LEADER'S GUIDE

Thank you for choosing to lead your group through this Bible study from Dr. Charles F. Stanley on *Experiencing Forgiveness.* The rewards of being a leader are different from those of participating, and it is our prayer that your own walk with Jesus will be deepened by this experience. During the twelve lessons in this study, you will be helping group members explore key themes related to the topic of forgiving themselves, forgiving others, and seeking forgiveness themselves through teachings by Dr. Charles Stanley and review questions that will encourage group discussion. There are multiple components in this section that can help you structure your lessons and discussion time, so please be sure to read and consider each one.

BEFORE YOU BEGIN

Before your first meeting, make sure your group members each have a copy of *Experiencing Forgiveness* so they can follow along in the study guide and have their answers written out ahead of time. Alternately, you can hand out the study guides at your first meeting and give the group members some time to look over the material and ask any preliminary questions. During your first meeting, be sure to send a sheet around the room and have the members write down their name, phone number, and email address so you can keep in touch with them during the week.

To ensure everyone has a chance to participate in the discussion, the ideal size for a group is around eight to ten people. If there are more than ten people, break up the bigger group into smaller subgroups. Make sure the members are committed to participating each week, as this will help create stability and help you better prepare the structure of the meeting.

At the beginning of each meeting, you may wish to start the group time by asking the group members to provide their initial reactions to the material they have read during the week. The goal is to just get the group members' preliminary thoughts—so encourage them at this point to keep their answers brief. Ideally, you want everyone in the group to get a chance to share some of their thoughts, so try to keep the responses to a minute or less.

Give the group members a chance to answer, but tell them to feel free to pass if they wish. With the rest of the study, it's generally not a good idea to have everyone answer every question—a free-flowing discussion is more desirable. But with the opening icebreaker questions, you can go around the circle. Encourage shy people to share, but don't force them. Also, try to keep any one person from dominating the discussion so everyone will have the opportunity to participate.

Weekly Preparation

As the group leader, there are a few things you can do to prepare for each meeting:

- *Be thoroughly familiar with the material in the lesson.* Make sure you understand the content of each lesson so you know how to structure the group time and are prepared to lead the group discussion.

- *Decide, ahead of time, which questions you want to discuss.* Depending on how much time you have each week, you may not be able to reflect on every question. Select specific questions you feel will evoke the best discussion.

- *Take prayer requests.* At the end of your discussion, be sure to take prayer requests from your group members and then pray for one another.

- *Pray for your group.* Pray for your group members throughout the week and ask that God would lead them as they study His Word.

- *Bring extra supplies to your meeting.* The members should bring their own pens for writing notes, but it's a good idea to have extras available for those who forget. You may also want to bring paper and additional Bibles.

Structuring the Group Discussion Time

You will need to determine with your group how long you want to meet each week so you can plan your time accordingly. Generally, most groups like to meet for either sixty minutes or ninety minutes, so you could use one of the following schedules:

Section	**60 Minutes**	**90 Minutes**
Welcome (group members arrive and get settled)	5 minutes	10 minutes
Icebreaker (group members share their initial thoughts regarding the content in the lesson)	10 minutes	15 minutes
Discussion (discuss the Bible study questions you selected ahead of time)	35 minutes	50 minutes
Prayer/Closing (pray together as a group and dismiss)	10 minutes	15 minutes

As the group leader, it is up to you to keep track of the time and keep things moving according to your schedule. If your group is having a good discussion, don't feel the need to stop and move on to the next question. Remember, the purpose is to pull together ideas and share unique insights on the lesson. Encourage everyone to participate, but don't be concerned if certain group members are more quiet. They may just be internally reflecting on the questions and need time to process their ideas before they can share them.

GROUP DYNAMICS

Leading a group study can be a rewarding experience for you and your group members—but that doesn't mean there won't be challenges. Certain members may feel uncomfortable in discussing topics that they consider very personal and might be afraid of being called on. Some members might have disagreements on specific issues. To help prevent these scenarios, consider establishing the following ground rules:

- If someone has a question that may seem off topic, suggest that it is discussed at another time, or ask the group if they are okay with addressing that topic.

- If someone asks a question to which you do not know the answer, confess that you don't know and move on. If you feel comfortable, you can invite the other group members to give their opinions or share their comments based on personal experience.

- If you feel like a couple of people are talking much more than others, direct questions to people who may not have shared yet. You could even ask the more dominating members to help draw out the quiet ones.

- When there is a disagreement, encourage the members to process the matter in love. Invite members from opposing sides to evaluate their opinions and consider the ideas of the other members. Lead the group through Scripture that addresses the topic, and look for common ground.

When issues arise, encourage your group to follow these words from Scripture: "Love one another" (John 13:34), "If it is possible, as much as it depends on you, live peaceably with all men" (Romans 12:18), "Whatever things are true . . . noble . . . pure . . . lovely . . . if there is any virtue and if there is anything praiseworthy—meditate on these things" (Philippians 4:8), and "Be swift to hear, slow to speak, slow to wrath" (James 1:19). This will make your group time more rewarding and beneficial for everyone who attends.

Thank you again for your willingness to lead your group. May God reward your efforts and dedication, equip you to guide your group in the weeks ahead, and make your time together in *Experiencing Forgiveness* fruitful for His kingdom.

Also Available in the Charles F. Stanley Bible Study Series

The Charles F. Stanley Bible Study Series is a unique approach to Bible study, incorporating biblical truth, personal insights, emotional responses, and a call to action. Each study draws on Dr. Stanley's many years of teaching the guiding principles found in God's Word, showing how we can apply them in practical ways to every situation we face. This edition of the series has been completely revised and updated, and includes two brand-new lessons from Dr. Stanley.

Advancing Through Adversity	Experiencing Forgiveness	Listening to God	Relying on the Holy Spirit
9780310106555	9780310106579	9780310106593	9780310106616

Available now at your favorite bookstore.
More volumes coming soon.